Watch out, watch out
Redundancy Crusader about!

I'm sure most of you will be way too young to remember this, but you'll get the idea anyway. In the 1970s, milk company Unigate ran a series of TV ads featuring characters called the Humphreys. The slogan 'Watch out, watch out – there's a Humphrey about' soon became a catchphrase.

The Humphreys were actually milk thieves but the only trace of themselves they ever left behind was a red and white striped straw. Four decades on, red and white are my crusading colours, and you can watch out, watch out for the Redundancy Crusader at:

- www.redundancycrusader.co.uk where you can access a free download, read my regular redundancy blogs, search the blog archive, and join the community and the debate;

- @elaine_hopkins on Twitter for life and redundancy tips, inspirational sayings and links;

- Elaine Hopkins on YouTube;

- www.redundancywithrespect.com where individuals and organizations that want to change their experience of redundancy can find out about coaching and workshops;

- Redundancy Crusader on Facebook; and

- Elaine Hopkins on LinkedIn.

I look forward to engaging with you there.

About 'Redundancy Sucks!'…

'My redundancy hit me hard. I wasn't expecting it and it hurt. I thought I'd always feel wounded, but Elaine coached me out of that and helped me find the inner resources I needed to get myself back into corporate life. Elaine's used a lot of the stuff in this book with me and it really works.'
Redundancy coaching client

'It is easy to forget the real emotions and experiences that individuals caught on the wrong end of redundancy endure. I will keep this book on my desk when designing redundancy exercises to inspire me to remember to do the least harm that I can and to help me explain to the people I work with how things feel when compliance is HR's only goal.'
Annabel Kaye – Managing Director of Irenicon, a specialist employment law and HR consultancy (www.irenicon.co.uk)

'What I love about this book is that Elaine takes us on a journey. It's as though we've crashed in the redundancy ditch and Elaine comes along on a tandem and picks us up. In Part I, she sits in front and steers the bike for us while teaching us loads of useful stuff. In Part 2, we steer the bike for ourselves, but Elaine is in the saddle behind supporting us as we try things out for ourselves. In Parts 3 and 4, we wobble away on our own, but with encouragement from the side of the road, as we hear how others have learned to ride the rocky road of redundancy. If you want to ride through the cycle of redundancy and come out the other side in good shape, then buy this book. I wish I'd had a copy when I went through it.'
Kathy Reid, Playwright

'You cannot always control what happens to you in life but you do have 100% control as to how you respond to it. Sometimes, especially when we are feeling stuck, we forget how powerful we are. Elaine's book is a valuable resource for people who have faced or are facing redundancy and who need support to boost their confidence and turn this life challenge into a life changing opportunity. This book should be compulsory reading for everyone involved in redundancy – from policy makers and employers to those experiencing the realities of being let go.'
Murielle Maupoint, Author of The Essential NLP Practitioner's Handbook and Founder of www.liveit.com

'Elaine presents perspectives and solutions in this book that will help anyone going through redundancy or unemployment. Actually, the wisdom Elaine expresses will help anyone at any time.'
Matthew Ferguson – Trainer of Hypnotherapy and NLP at Motivation Training (www.motivationtraining.co.uk)

'This book is the next best thing to being coached by Elaine. On *Masterchef*, contestants sometimes say "That's me on a plate". This is Elaine in a book: warm, wise and witty. Best of all, parts of the book are laugh out loud funny – and I wasn't expecting that.'
Redundancy Coaching Client

'As a serial survivor, I wish I'd had this book earlier in life. I've been through a number of self-imposed redundancies when I had to sell successful businesses to accommodate my changing lifestyle. Those experiences would have been so much easier if I'd known then what I know now – thanks to Elaine's book. I've made so many notes in it that I'm going to have to buy myself another copy!'
Louise Heasman – Founder of modern day marketing! (www.moderndaymarketing.co.uk)

'Since being made redundant 20 years ago, I've discovered not only the power of NLP but also my true purpose in life. The discovery of both would have been so much easier if I'd had this book to hand.'
Olive Hickmott – Founder of www.empoweringlearning.co.uk and Author

'Here's how to get back in the driving seat. In this very practical book, Elaine has taken the tools I gave her and applied them to one of life's big challenges. If you want to create a life of your choosing, start reading…'
Ian McDermott – Founder of International Teaching Seminars (www.itsnlp.com)

Redundancy Sucks!

AN NLP GUIDE TO SURVIVING AND THRIVING AFTER THE AXE

ELAINE HOPKINS

AKA The Redundancy Crusader

lip

First published in 2012 by:

Live It Publishing
27 Old Gloucester Road
London, United Kingdom.
WC1N 3AX
www.liveitpublishing.com

Copyright © 2012 by Elaine Hopkins
Illustrations by Caroline Chapple

Although every effort has been made to ensure the accuracy of the information, advice and instructions contained in this book, it is sold with the understanding that neither the author nor the publisher are giving specific advice. Each reader may have unique needs and circumstances that can present complex issues that are beyond the scope of this book. For individual advice, please consult a coach, therapist or specialist redundancy consultant.

All case study scenarios and results are real, but the author has changed names and identifying characteristics of those featured in the book to protect their identities, unless they have given their permission to be identified.

ISBN 978-1-906954-55-0 (pbk)

With heartfelt thanks to the people who made me redundant and unwittingly led me to my destiny.

To Annabel
Thank you for being one of my 'three wise women' and for all those hours in the 'Rayon d'Or.' Elaine /x

Acknowledgements

As with so much else in life, the Beatles often sum it up best. In my case, it's been an excessively 'long and winding road' that's brought me here.

Now that I've paused momentarily, I'm sending a huge thank you to all who had a hand in the birthing of this book, in particular:

CDH for his continuing inspiration;

Ann Cottis, Dee Cullen, Marc Hommel, David Prosser, Ed Wilson and Gillian Windett for noticing and nurturing my potential;

Matt Ferguson, Art Giser and Ian McDermott for their training genius;

John Mushens for being the best natural teacher I could ever hope to encounter;

Teak Rehman for his real and realistic coaching;

Louise Heasman for her marketing and hand-holding genius;

Caroline Chapple for adorning my words with her creative genius;

Annabel Kaye for her glorious generosity in initiating me into the mysteries of HR and the law;

Murielle Maupoint and Dorothy Newton for showing me a better way and for giving me hope for the future;

Naomi Lowde and Kathy Reid for being such inspirational and creative trail-blazers;

Alexey Kuzmin for his bravery and generosity in volunteering;

Jason Browne for his challenging support;

Nick Williams of Inspired Entrepreneur for lightening the load of resistance and facilitating epiphanies;

Mark Forrest of Classic FM for his matutinal musical motivation;

all the exceptional interviewees who gave so freely of their time, talents and thoughts;

all my coaching clients who teach and inspire me as we go along;

my family of friends for their love, laughter and occasional stern word; and

Gill Pullen for accompanying me on the journey, especially during those frequent intervals when she had no idea where I was going – and frankly, my dear, neither did I.

I am in the debt of you all; and it feels good. As for any mistakes, misrepresentations, misunderstandings, I'm going to be selfish with those: they're all mine.

Contents

Foreword by Olive Hickmott   1

How This Book Began   3

First Things First   5

PART I: **GETTING OVER REDUNDANCY**   11

Chapter I: Reviewing the situation   13

Chapter II: Transitioning out and in   15

Chapter III: Getting in the right state   27

Chapter IV: Navigating our map of the world   37

Chapter V: Exploring our belief system   49

Chapter VI: Minding our Ps and Qs   57

Chapter VII: Mining our resources   69

Chapter VIII: Finding our flexibility   79

Chapter IX: Taking a trip down our timeline   89

Chapter X: Having a spring clean   99

PART II: **GETTING ON WITH THE REST OF OUR LIFE**   107

Chapter XI: Being who we are   109

Chapter XII: Learning to inkle   119

Chapter XIII: Working out what we really, really want   129

Chapter XIV: Getting our strategies straight   143

Chapter XV: Building more rapport   157

Chapter XVI: Perfecting our plasticity   167

PART III: **PROFESSIONAL PERSPECTIVES**   181

Chapter XVII: Why is redundancy so often conducted in a
                      less than ideal manner?   183

Chapter XVIII: Is there a different model of redundancy
                  already out there? The charitable sector:
                  take one.   193
Chapter XIX: Is there a different model of redundancy
                  already out there? The charitable sector:
                  take two.   201

PART IV: **REDUNDANCY STORIES**   207
Chapter XX: Aleksandr   209
Chapter XXI: Cathy   213
Chapter XXII: Darcy   219
Chapter XXIII: Joanna   225
Chapter XXIV: Marie   231
Chapter XXV: Naomi   235
Chapter XXVI: Paul   239
Chapter XXVII: Rebecca   245
Chapter XXVIII: Will   251

How This Book Doesn't End – Yet   257
References   259
Glossary   263
About the Author   269
Index   271

Foreword

Redundancy is a very sad, very real fact of life that's affecting more and more people. We may never know the true toll of the effects of redundancy. What we do know is that they can be extreme. We do not have to search the media for very long before we come across a story about the devastating impact of redundancy on everyday life.

The statistics are horrendous. According to the Chartered Institute of Personnel and Development[1]:

- nearly 2.7 million people have been made redundant in the UK in the past three years;

- that has cost the nation, in terms of lost output, £135 billion, or 10% of GDP;

- the cost to UK employers is staggering – £35 billion.

These figures are so overwhelming that we can drown in them. But, if we do that, we lose sight of one very important fact: behind each of these numbers is a very personal story, a very personal loss. Moreover, it's a loss that ripples outwards to families, friends, former colleagues, whole communities.

A swift incursion into the internet reveals that most of the available help relates to legal rights, benefits, career counselling, outplacement services, schemes and courses. Elaine's take on redundancy is somewhat different. She has set out on a crusade both to empower those made redundant to help themselves and to identify a better model of redundancy for employers. I know that for her this book is just the beginning of a passionate quest.

As someone whose life purpose is to use NLP to help people overcome their difficulties – whether they be related to dyslexia, dyspraxia, dyscalculia, ADHD, autism, Asperger's or Tourette's – I feel a close connection with Elaine's crusade. I am also profoundly honoured to be writing this foreword.

My clients don't deserve their learning difficulties; you don't deserve your redundancy. That's enough of a link for me, but there's an even better one. I too have experienced redundancy: 20 years ago, I was made redundant from my post as research and development director in a hi-tech company. I can honestly say that it was the best thing that ever happened to me.

The process was terrible, but letting go of all that launched me into a world of self-discovery, great success and, above all, fun. I exploited the skills I already had, and took the opportunity to learn new ones. Together, these enabled me to create a hugely rewarding life, doing a job I love. And the message I always pass on to people in this situation is to take redundancy as an opportunity to find a role that you're passionate about and that you enjoy.

Since my redundancy, I've worked with thousands of families, transforming their lives in ways they hadn't even considered possible. I've also published four books. This is the magic and mystery of NLP – a magic and mystery that can help you transform your experience of redundancy. Let this book show you how.

Olive Hickmott
Director, International Association for Health and Learning
Founder and Owner of Empowering Health and Empowering Learning
Author of 'Bridges to Success – How to Transform Learning Difficulties', 'Recover Your Energy', 'You Too Can Do Health' and 'Seeing Spells Achieving'

How This Book Began

It's the 18th of June, 2010. I'm sitting in a large conference room, confronted by two people, one of whom I count as a friend. But there's nothing friendly about this encounter. The organization for which I have worked for nine years has no further need of me. That I understand and accept. What I do not understand and accept is the way in which it has chosen to dispose of me.

The other two people set the tone of the meeting. It's hostile and disrespectful, so hostile and disrespectful in fact that I feel ashamed: not of myself, for I have done nothing wrong, but of my employer. I stay in the conference room only until I think I've spotted a flaw in the redundancy process. Then I leave the room and the organization, but – with the help of an employment lawyer – on my terms.

Those ten minutes in that room lead me to my destiny. Its first manifestation is Woody the Woodpecker. He's hammering out a message in my head. It never varies, just continues insistently: *redundancy with respect, redundancy with respect* over and over and over again.

I become adept at tuning Woody out because I have other concerns. How am I going to earn a decent living, rather than just survive? I manage to ignore him for a whole four months. Then, because I'm a great believer in gut instinct, I realize that if Woody is being so annoyingly insistent, his message is probably worth the airtime.

I surrender and set up www.redundancywithrespect.com. At least the hammering stops. I become busy with my freelance copywriting and coaching activities, and Woody's moved on from my head, so that's

3

OK. Except my head isn't OK, because I have a near-fatal accident while cycling the pilgrim route in northern Spain.

Five months after the accident, I realize that I didn't die that day because I still have my destiny to fulfil. My mission in life is to use all my skills as a copywriter, coach and hypnotherapist to one end: to help you to get over redundancy and get on with the rest of your life.

That's why this book and my websites exist, and why Woody wouldn't go away.

First Things First

This book is something of a hybrid: practical guide + professional perspectives + redundancy stories. There's one very good reason for that: redundancy is a personal issue, even when our employers (crassly, in my opinion) tell us not to take it personally, but it's also a corporate and a societal issue. Why do so many employers choose to conduct redundancy in a manner that leaves their ex-employees feeling bereft – not just of their job, but of so much else?

Thanks to the numerous people I've interviewed, I now have many more insights into the answer to that question, but my righteous anger about the topic remains. Not only does it remain, it now burns at an even higher combustion rate. I wasn't the Redundancy Crusader when I started writing this book, but I definitely am now. For more on my crusading activities, see the beginning of this book.

When I was a child and watched cowboy series on our newly acquired television set, there was usually gold in *them thar hill*s. There's certainly nuggets of gold, pearls of wisdom, thoughts for the day in the redundancy stories in part IV of this book. They cover a wide range: some happened a while ago; some are so current that they don't have a resolution – yet.

I've included them because stories are both important and powerful, as demonstrated by their long history and their universality. They can instruct, inspire and influence on both a conscious and unconscious level. What you make of the stories included here is up to you.

The book's prime purpose though is as a how-to manual: how to help you to get over redundancy so that you can get on with the rest of your life. We don't know exactly what that's going to involve, but I can take a pretty shrewd guess that it may well require you to do things differently from how you've always done them.

There's some good news coming next: there's a tool that can help you with that. It's called NLP (Neuro-Linguistic Programming). The official definition is: 'the study of the structure of subjective experience', but somehow that doesn't do it for me. I prefer to think of it as the essential how-to tool. If I keep on referring to NLP, it's for one simple and very good reason: it works.

So does other stuff, and I've included anything that I've found useful as I've helped myself and others to emerge from the dark side of redundancy. This includes the work of Martin Seligman, one of the major contributors to Positive Psychology and sponsor of the 'Values in Action' surveys referred to in this book.

Back to NLP: since first learning about it in 2004, I've used it to transform my life from the inside out. Most importantly, it's enabled me to understand myself and to change those aspects that used to drive me mad, those aspects that I really didn't want in my life.

I write about myself a fair bit in this book. Not because I'm an *it's all about me* person; far from it. I've spent most of my time on the planet being absent from my own life. Now that I'm fully engaged, I want you to understand just how radically you can change your daily existence. In terms of show and tell, I believe showing to be far more powerful than telling; the best way that I can show you is by referring to my own experience with NLP.

Given that in the how-to part of this book we'll be beginning, middling and ending with you, being equipped with a tool that enables you to understand and change yourself (if you want) is fairly fundamental.

NLP began life in the US in the 1970s. The co-developers were Richard Bandler, a psychology student, and John Grinder, an associate professor of linguistics. Their original stimulus was the desire to identify *the difference that makes the difference* between therapists such as Milton Erikson, Fritz Perls, and Virginia Satir who had very high success rates with their clients and other practitioners who didn't.

As Bandler and Grinder tested out ideas and insights on their friends, the creative group expanded and developed some key NLP concepts such as anchoring, representational systems, and reframing.

Essentially, NLP is based on four pillars (so named by Ian McDermott):

- rapport – meeting other people in their model of the world;

- sensory acuity – noticing the effects of what we do, on ourselves and on others;

- outcome orientation – knowing what we want and checking that we're using appropriate behaviour to achieve it; and

- behavioural flexibility – realizing that we always have more than one choice.

Just take a minute to read through those again; they could have been designed to help us tackle redundancy.

NLP includes a number of presuppositions. These are guidelines based on human experience of what works. I've included one with each chapter as our presupposition du jour (PDJ). My model here is the menu du jour so favoured by restaurants: just pick what you fancy.

If the only thing you take away with you from this book is these presuppositions strung together as a daisy chain, you will already have the wherewithal to radically change the way you live – each and every day of your life.

Explaining NLP in all its glory is way beyond the scope of this book. When you want to investigate further, 'Neuro-linguistic Programming for Dummies'[2] is probably the most accessible primer. Alternatively, find yourself a course. I did all my training with ITS[3].

You don't need an in-depth knowledge of NLP to understand this book. I've worked with dozens of coaching clients without ever using those three initials. I've included some of their stories to add colour and broaden your understanding. My coaching clients are ordinary people just like you and me; well, ordinary in the sense that they're uniquely talented human beings, but are also work in progress. I've also included a glossary and some basic information about NLP as we go along for the curious among you.

It would, by the way, be an excellent idea to start introducing more curiosity into your daily life. We're about to embark on a voyage of self-discovery, so why not get curious about one thing about yourself each day? Just start noticing your reactions: why do you react so sharply to a certain tone of voice or word; with such pleasure to a certain aroma?

If you're truly prepared to engage with NLP to discover more about yourself, it can be fast, fun, easy – and life-changing. The one thing it isn't though is a left brain, logical activity. We're going to be working with two of the most powerful forces known to mankind: memory and imagination.

I'll be asking you to do some stuff that may initially seem, sound and feel weird. I think this initially weird category only exists because we've largely lost the habit of paying attention to our own inner experience. We're often encouraged to *vent our spleen* or *let it all out*, but getting our innermost feelings on the outside and leaving them there is absolutely not the same as going inside ourselves, acknowledging what we find there and working with it.

So yes, I will be asking you to notice your own experience: from listening to your inner dialogue, to locating where in your body a particular feeling sits, to conducting conversations with various parts of yourself. All I can do is crave your indulgence. After all, if you're reading this book because you're experiencing redundancy, then you may well have very little to lose but an awful lot to gain by learning more about yourself.

Nothing in this book can possibly do you any harm. I'm only going to issue two caveats.

One: use your common sense about when and where you practise. Shortly after we learned NLP, friend John and I decided to play around with our timelines (see chapter IX) while waiting to order in a restaurant. We came back to the external world to find a waitress tapping her foot and giving us a very strange look. I also overshot my destination on several train journeys because I was so deeply immersed.

Two: learn to pace yourself. You'll be engaging with yourself in a different way, using parts of your brain that may have lain dormant for a while. As a result, you may feel unusually tired and have very vivid dreams. This is absolutely normal; just listen to your body. When it tells you that it's had enough for one day, heed its warning.

Following along will be childishly easy if you become as a child. Remember that spirit of playfulness and acceptance, that readiness to try anything, that ability to laugh and smile when things don't work out quite as you'd planned and, as Lew Stone so aptly has it:

pick yourself up, dust yourself down, and start all over again.

That's exactly what we're going for: the best role model I can give you is a toddler learning to walk. Imagine the scene: the toddler manages to get to his feet, balance precariously, take a tottering step or two, and fall down on his bottom, smiling and giggling, but with an absolute determination to try again. Forget all that adult stuff about being afraid to make a mistake, always having to be right, judging yourself against others, having to get it right first time.

In this book, there is no right or wrong, no failure or success; all there is your experience, your feedback, and your willingness to use both as you discover and shape your new niche in life.

Part I

Getting Over Redundancy

Chapter I

Reviewing the situation

PDJ

We're all doing the best we can,

given the circumstances.

Confronting the harsh reality of redundancy is horrible, difficult, and every other negative adjective you can bring to mind. There are two concepts though that can help us to begin our journey from where we are to where we want to be.

I: We haven't lost our job

I've spent over 30 years as a copywriter in corporate life, so I'm a huge fan of words but even I would have to admit that, in the case of redundancy, the English language doesn't do us any favours. Unless we've had our fingers in the till, been grossly inflating our expense claims, or committed any other form of misconduct, we haven't lost our job. We've had it taken away from us. If, as predicted, there are going to be more than 300,000 redundancies in the next five years in the public sector alone, then we need to adopt this as our mantra.

But that's just the first part of the mantra. We may not be responsible for the loss of our job, but we are absolutely 100% responsible for how we react to that loss. So let's promise ourselves right here and right now that we're going to live up to that responsibility and take it seriously.

When our job is taken away, we all suffer at least two losses: work and income. Some of us lose so much more: comradeship, routine, meaning, self-confidence, self-worth. This is no different – except perhaps in scale – from when we lose someone that we love. We have a perfect right to feel all those emotions: that bewildering mix of anger, grief, self-pity, resentment, guilt – all overlaid with a sense of why me?

Experience those emotions by all means but, sooner rather than later, it's going to be time to bid them farewell. They're all negative, and negative emotions can be really, really draining and we're going to need all our energy for what lies ahead.

II: We are so much more than our job-title

Have you ever noticed how often people tell you what they are when you ask them what they do?

What do you do?

I'm a lab assistant...marketing exec...operations manager...retail buyer...high class call girl.

Except in our case, we're an ex-whatever. No, we're not. We may have had our job taken away from us, but we are still the same unique and uniquely talented person we were the day before that happened. Our identity (who we are) is most emphatically not the same as our behaviour (what we do or, in our case, used to do).

Chapter II

Transitioning from and to

PDJ

We aren't broken, so we don't need fixing.

OK, so we've been made redundant. All that means is that our employers have no further use for us. And they've probably made their decision on very limited information. We're all far more multi-talented and resourceful than most employers realize.

So let's make use of that resourcefulness right now to make sure that we're starting from the right point. My father was fond of saying that if you wanted to go to Bristol, then the first step was to get yourself to Paddington and buy a ticket. Yes, I know it's ridiculously simple, but it's also true that we can all be so busy concentrating on our destination that we completely ignore our departure point.

I believe this is particularly the case when it comes to transitions. This is just a fancy word for all those points in our life when we change from one status to another: child to adolescent, adolescent to adult, learner to earner, single to married, adult to parent, married to divorced, straight to gay, employed to unemployed, alive to dead.

Unless we're either extremely confused or exceptionally unlucky or both, we won't be experiencing all of those in any one lifetime. We will all be experiencing some of them though, which highlights the fact that they're inevitable, unavoidable milestones in our life. They're also occasions when we move from one set of circumstances to another. That's why it's important to pay just as much attention to the *from* phase as the *to* one.

In fact, life without transitions would be unbearably dull because we'd never develop or change or become more than we were when we arrived on the planet. Not all transitions are the same of course: some we welcome with open arms; others we try and avoid as we would the plague.

Now may well be a good point for you to cast your mind back to the other transitions in your life. What can you learn from those previous experiences that will help you here?

Let's acknowledge that we're dealing with a particularly unwelcome transition – the one from employment to unemployment, but at least we are dealing with it. So how can we make sure that we're at the right departure point? Given that, on average, a human being can only hold a very limited number of items in working memory, I've limited my suggestions to five:

1 Take time out for yourself

You can picture me climbing onto my soapbox for this one. That's why it's first in the list. It operates on three levels: personal, practical and systemic.

Personal

When we get made redundant from a job, we get inundated with advice; it's coming at us from all directions – Job Centre, employment lawyer, recruitment consultant, outplacement advisor. In fact, it's coming at us so fast and furiously that we lose the opportunity to just be, to give ourselves some time and space in which to come to terms with what's happened. If we want to have any sense of control whatsoever over what comes next – whatever that may be, we really need to make time for ourselves at the very beginning.

The bevy of advisors have our best interests at heart and are doing all they can for us. Of course they are, but there's a time and a place for them and it comes later.

In terms of stress, losing our job ranks right up there with bereavement and divorce. There's simply no point in under-estimating the enormous demands that unwelcome transitions can make on our body, mind and spirit. They can seriously weaken our immune system, leaving us open to illness and infection.

With all this going on, sleep assumes even more importance than usual. Although individual requirements differ, experts agree that eight hours per night is optimal, with less than six and more than ten being positively harmful. Sleep not only reinforces the immune system and allows the body to recover, it also provides an important opportunity for mental processing.

Finally, I find song titles and choruses an unending source of wisdom, so do remember that:

a little of what you fancy does you good.

We're using this as a reminder to reward ourselves with an occasional treat that makes us feel good; no need to embrace the sexual undertones with which mischievous music hall performer Marie Lloyd imbued the song – unless, of course, that's your idea of a proper treat. In which case, the rest of us will just leave you to it.

Practical

On a practical level, you're going to have less income than before, even if you've been fortunate enough to receive a substantial pay-out. Calculating your personal or family survival budget is therefore a must.

I'm not going to pretend to you either that I'm a financial expert or that I spent months existing on bread and water and in imminent danger of my house being re-possessed. I'm not and I didn't. If you are in that unfortunate position, it won't improve by itself. Recognize the gravity of the situation and seek help and advice now.

During my redundancy, I spent a fair few months existing on one-third of my previous income. That taught me two valuable lessons: there's a distinct difference between what we need and what we want; and a surprising number of goods and services are available for free, at reduced rates or by bartering.

There may also be other matters (school fees, discretionary spending, gap years, pets, second car, club memberships, holidays) that you need to address sooner rather than later. Hasty decision-making in the wake of an unwelcome transition is probably not a great combination, but you do at least need to be alert to the possibility of a change of plans, and to alert the other parties involved as well.

Systemic

Systems thinking is no more than looking at an entity as a whole and understanding how its component parts influence one another. In our case, the entity concerned is the family, couple or group of which we're a part. Our redundancy is going to affect everyone in our system in ways both obvious and unexpected.

If the financial strain is the most obvious, the relationship strain may well be the most unexpected. And the stress points sometimes show up in the most unexpected places.

One of my clients – a high-flier in his late 30s – simply couldn't cope with the fact that his partner kept interrupting him when they were both at home. He was used to strictly segmenting and allocating his time, completing tasks methodically, having absolute control over his own agenda. The mutual love between him and his partner was never in doubt; their ability to spend their days together in the same house definitely was.

If you're going to be an unaccustomed presence in a household that runs to its own version of clockwork without you, then be aware of that. Also, be sensitive about what you see as its shortcomings.

When my father – whose background was in organization and methods – retired, he decided to accompany my mother on her shopping trips. Apparently, she'd been doing the shopping in the wrong way for the past 40 years. Although she took it in good part and allowed him to compile the list in aisle order and pack the basket on wheels in reverse order of unpacking, she also encouraged him to find other ways of expressing his business acumen.

Getting everyone in your system together to discuss and reach mutual agreement on some reasonable and respectful ground rules that everyone can abide by could be a useful first step. From then on, it's largely a question of monitoring what's working and adjusting what isn't.

2 Pay particular attention to your physical and mental well-being

Losing our job often means that we also lose our accustomed daily routine. We can, however, craft ourselves a new one. Ideally, let's arrange our days such that we engage our mind, body and other people.

Even if you've had to give up your gym membership temporarily, you can still go out walking, running or biking for free. Vast quantities of mental stimulation are also readily available – from crosswords in free newspapers to lectures at local libraries, museums and art galleries. As for other people, you can find them at the end of a phone line and at the click of a send button, even if they're not present physically. It's really important to stay connected with your network.

Make a point too of eating well and regularly, even if your appetite goes haywire in the first few days.

We'll come onto role models in chapter VII. In the meantime, here's a negative one. What you don't want is to become a junk-food-addicted couch potato who spends hours in front of assorted electronic gadgets. There are lots of reasons why you don't want to get off on the wrong unhealthy foot. I list just two of them below.

Excessive television viewing can contribute to mild depression through the effects of comparing ourselves with the 'ideals' portrayed, objectification, boredom, an emphasis on consumerism, less sleep, less exercise, and more social isolation. Nor does the internet get a rave review in this respect. Technology writer Nicholas Carr believes that prolonged use of the worldwide web may reduce our capacity to concentrate, contemplate and create[4]. Enough of this nanny state stuff; it's so not my style.

3 Find yourself a project

This one sounds counter-cultural I know, but it'll pay dividends in the end. Redundancy often leaves us feeling bruised, battered, out of sorts. One way of lifting our spirits is to do something – anything – that we find engaging and comforting. Turning the activity into a project will make it more satisfying and meaningful.

Apart from anything else, you're going to be venturing far beyond the bounds of your established comfort zone, so having an enjoyable project already up and running can only be a good thing. You can retreat into its comforting space if there are times when being in transition threatens to overwhelm you.

Bizarre at it may sound, my project was gaining an 'A' Level in Spanish. Did I need another 'A' Level? At my age, I think not. But I'm a life-long learner and a word junkie, so it suited me down to the ground. It also gave me two other opportunities: to fit in some extra exercise by cycling to college, and to meet a new group of people. Moreover, if you're still in receipt of Jobseeker's Allowance, discounts on college fees can be substantial.

4 Make optimism and laughter a daily habit

If the last one sounded counter-cultural, this one must sound completely off the wall. Bear with me: there's some good stuff on how to manage your state coming right up in the next chapter. In the meantime, let's just start with Dr Carl Simonton's premise that:

In the absence of certainty, there is nothing wrong with hope.

Not only is there nothing wrong with hope, there's a great deal right with it. In fact, there's a link between optimism and good health that operates across diverse cultures and conditions (asthma, heart disease, fatigue, rheumatoid arthritis), and also influences healthy ageing and longevity.[5] It's also true that there's a genetic influence on our disposition towards optimism or pessimism[6], but we can't keep blaming our parents for everything. Nor do we need to head down that well-worn track again, even if we agree with Philip Larkin that:

they f**k you up, your mum and dad.

If you do tend towards pessimism and want to explore further, *Learned Optimism*[7] by Martin Seligman, one of the major contributors to Positive Psychology, is probably the best place to go. For now, rest assured that you can build your optimistic ability just by recognizing your pessimistic thoughts for what they are and then disputing them. Seligman advises us to:

Treat them [your own pessimistic thoughts] as if they were uttered by an external person, a rival whose mission in life was to make you miserable.[8]

He advocates the ABCDE model in which:

A = the adversity that's prompted the pessimistic thought;

B = the automatic beliefs that accompany such adversity;

C = the usual consequences of those beliefs;

D = the disputation of those routine beliefs; and

E = the energization that follows successful disputation.

By effectively disputing the beliefs that follow an adversity, you can change your reaction from dejection and giving up to activity and good cheer.[8]

You can also get into the habit of asking yourself:

What's the worst that can happen?

As a general rule, it's nowhere near as bad as your worst imaginings and can sometimes be relatively trivial. For good measure, you can invoke Mark Twain who said of himself:

My life has been filled with calamities, some of which actually happened.

As for the connection between laughter and health, this goes back to Biblical times at least:

A merry heart doeth good like a medicine: but a broken spirit drieth the bones. [9]

Medical science can now confirm Solomon's proverbial wisdom. There are well-established links between laughter and the healthy function of blood vessels,[10] a reduction in stress hormones and the release of endorphins that can relieve some physical pain,[11] and the development of a stronger immune system.[12]

As with learning to walk, laughter is another example where children lead the field. I haven't been able to find any research to confirm this, but it's alleged that young children laugh up to 300 times a day. In contrast, by the time we reach 40, the number has dropped to four.

During redundancy, let's aim to raise that number significantly. It doesn't matter how you do it: spend more time with the children in your family group, read cartoon strips, watch re-runs of 'Frasier'. Me, I re-read AA Milne's 'Winnie-the-Pooh' and 'The House at Pooh Corner'. Eeyore just cracks me up. Whatever presses your laughter button, turn it on – daily and repeatedly.

To help get you into the habit, I'm writing this book in a relatively light tone. Not because I'm under-estimating the seriousness of the situation but because, to misquote 'The Book of Common Prayer':

In the midst of life we are in laughter.

Believe you me, it can only help.

5 Get more yet into your life

For a three letter word, *yet* packs a powerful punch. I think it's inherently helpful because it allows us to cut ourselves some slack and to entertain the possibility of choice and change in the not too distant.

No, I haven't got over my redundancy yet (but that's OK).

No, I don't yet know what the next step is (out of all the possible steps).

No, I don't know yet how I'll be earning money (but I will at some stage).

No matter how many unwelcome transitions you've been through before, there's no guarantee that you're going to sail through this one in no time at all with barely a backward glance. Accept that and you'll be less likely to beat yourself up. Indulging in that unproductive activity will achieve nothing except decrease your resourcefulness and increase the likelihood of you falling ill.

Adopting a *yet* mentality allows you to choose how you view redundancy. It's absolutely OK not to be over it *yet*. There may well be very good reasons for that, but do you really want to be in that same position two years from now? How you view redundancy will fundamentally affect how you experience it.

Is it so drastic and life-threatening that you'll never ever get over it? A transition that gives you a chance to take stock, consider what you really want, and maybe set off on a whole new course? Or any of the myriad perspectives in between these two polarities?

Redundancy is an unwelcome transition, and yes, it can suck, but that's not the only thing it can do. As with any other situation not of our choosing, redundancy is either what we make of it or what we could make of it once we discover more about ourselves. The point of this book is to help you make that discovery, but you still need to choose a perspective that works for you.

Earlier on in this chapter, I referred to an unwelcome transition as a *milestone*. If we change just one letter of that word, it becomes *millstone*, used figuratively to refer to a heavy burden. *Milestone* or *millstone*: to a greater or lesser extent, it's our choice.

Chapter III

Getting in the right state

> ## PDJ
>
> *Experience has a structure.*

Let's start this chapter with a question:

So how are you?

When people ask us how we are, we tend to treat the question as more of a ritual than a serious enquiry. You know the kind of thing I mean. We see someone we know, we ask how they are, they respond briefly, then ask how we are, we respond briefly. Formalities over, now we can get on with the real guts of the conversation.

My *so how are you?* isn't one of those. It's both a serious question and the starting point for everything we'll be doing together.

As a general rule, we don't pay particularly close attention to what's happening on the inside. Usually, the first time that I ask my coaching clients:

What's happening on the inside?

they look completely bemused. We're simply not in the habit of realizing that we have a rich and rewarding inner experience that can also be immensely useful.

I, for one, blame René Descartes for he it was who decided that the mind and the body are two separate systems. Everyone is, of course, entitled to his or her own opinion. However, I can't help pondering the possibility that Descartes' penchant for spending so much time in a large, lovely, warm bread oven may possibly have addled his thinking.

Anyway, what we're talking about here are states. And we often talk about them in real life as well.

Ooh, she's in a right state.

If you say it in the *Ada* voice so beloved of British comic Les Dawson, the Lancashire accent makes it even funnier. But the fun masks a fundamental truth: we're all in some state every waking moment of our life. What state are you in right now? Are you angry, happy, sad, disgusted, fed up? Let's find out.

Settle yourself comfortably in a chair, plant your feet firmly on the floor, make yourself comfortable, take a couple of deep relaxing breaths, and close your eyes. Now, just notice how you are: what feelings you're experiencing, what pictures you're seeing in your mind's eye, what internal dialogue you're hearing.

What you've just done is examined your own state. Our state is a remarkably reliable indicator of the quality of our relationship with the world at large. It affects us on a neurological, physical, mental, emotional, energetic and spiritual level.

That's about as comprehensive a list of human power and potential as you can get. It's particularly impressive when you consider that most of the time we're not even consciously aware of our own state.

And guess what? All that power and potential is under your control. Yes, it's true: the only person in charge of your emotions and therefore your state is you. It seems blindingly obvious to me now, but I remember that it was a major revelation to me at the beginning of my long – and continuing – personal development.

I used to inhabit a world where if I woke up in a bad mood, that was it for the whole day. As George Gershwin so memorably and musically reminds us:

it ain't necessarily so.

In the immediate aftermath of redundancy, there are so many well-meaning people on our case from various agencies that it's all too easy to lose touch with ourselves.

After my redundancy, I had no idea what I wanted to do. Prompted by the Job Centre and the employment agency, I started trawling through the job ads on the Internet. I was half-way through a job description when I suddenly became aware of what was happening to my insides: they were shrinking with horror, and shrieking with terror:

Please, please, don't make us go back to the corporate crap.

Quite right too: been there; done that; ad nauseam. The habit of checking in with myself saved me from going down completely the wrong track. Just as a reminder, I still keep all my blogs and business-related stuff in the folder I named *Jobsearch* at a time when I was listening to other people, rather than to my own inner promptings.

What many of us don't realize is that we can control our own states and can change them at will. Yours has probably already shifted slightly, just by dint of examining it.

Before we go any further, let me just ask you one question:

What's your baseline state?

Your baseline state (so named by Ian McDermott) is the one in which you habitually hang out, to which you return in those precious moments of peace and quiet, and with which you are most familiar. The variations are endless: from low-level anxiety to incipient laughter. Take a few moments to identify and describe your baseline state.

If you don't particularly like your baseline state, if it gives you gloomy thoughts, makes you feel bad about yourself, makes you feel less able to do things, then you can change it for one that does the exact opposite.

You might want to start by becoming curious about other people's states. Whom would you pick as your role model? You can have great fun with this because the models don't have to be human. When I want to be in a state of complete and utter contentment and comfort, my model is a cat sleeping and stretching in a sunny spot.

My baseline state used to be fear that spiked and fell like the line on a cardiac monitor:

What would happen if I had to talk to someone I didn't know at the coffee machine?

What would I do if a director asked me to undertake a work project that was out of my (very limited) comfort zone?'

These days, my baseline state is a delightful mixture of rampant curiosity and barely suppressed laughter. A babbling brook has replaced the cardiac monitor. I used not to do curiosity at all for fear I might find out something I didn't want to know; now it's my dominant strength, as demonstrated by the *Values in Action Strengths Survey*[13] (of which more later – see chapter XI).

So how can you change your state? There's one very simple way: if you change your physiology, you will also change your state. Whatever your current position – standing, sitting, lying down – change it, and your state will automatically change. It will change even more dramatically if you indulge in some aerobic exercise for a couple of minutes.

I believe this is why research shows that walking relieves the symptoms of depression. Depressed people know exactly how to connect with their bad feelings about themselves and to conduct extremely negative internal dialogue. Both of these mental processes require a person to look down – not an activity we usually associate with the act of walking, especially if we're doing it in company.

It's a given in NLP that you can re-experience any state, even if you've only been in it once before in your entire life. Every state is associated both with the circumstances surrounding it (what you were doing, thinking, feeling, seeing, smelling, hearing, tasting) and with the label that you've given it: supreme confidence, say. Our memories establish a connexion between the circumstances and the state so that by recalling or triggering a particular memory we can re-create the associated state.

If you want to test this out for yourselves, just prick up your ears the next time you hear a song that has a particular significance for you and notice what happens on the inside. If you can't wait to try it out, know that the sound will take you back to the time in question and all the feelings you had then will come flooding back.

Redundancy may well have left you in an extremely negative state, particularly if your employer handled the process badly. I have a questionnaire that I go through with people who've experienced redundancy. One of the questions is:

What did your employer do well during the redundancy process?

So far, all the answers bar two have been *nothing*, but hope springs eternal.

Let's get back to the matter in hand. What would be a helpful state for you to be in as you tackle redundancy? It could be that heady mixture of self-belief, confidence and sure-footedness that you have when you're at your very best – on those days when you don't seem able to put a foot wrong.

It's a particularly good example because when you have it, it's just second nature and you don't question it. When you don't have it, you can't imagine where you're going to find it. The answer, my friends, is within. This is a state that belongs to you; it's part of your history because you've experienced it before. All you have to do now is find it.

So put what you're looking for into words, ask yourself when you were in that state, and just see what comes to mind. As with so much else in NLP, this isn't really a matter of consciously trying; just notice what floats into the forefront of your mind. Bear in mind too that when, where or in what context you had the experience is of absolutely no consequence.

Having identified the most appropriate previous experience, just re-live it in a totally associated state ie you're fully in your body and looking out of your own eyes. Make the experience as vivid as you can – see what you see, hear what you hear, feel what you feel. This mental activity will trigger physiological changes in your body. As your posture, breathing, pulse, heart rate and muscle tone subtly change, so too does your internal state. Once you're in your desired state, anchor it in some way.

You could, for example, either press your thumb and forefinger together, or create a visual image, or say a word silently to yourself. What you've just done is created an anchor for yourself of you at your very best. You may well need to use your anchor in public situations, so remember to make it something that's both portable and discreet.

You don't want other candidates waiting with you for a job interview wondering why you keep performing the Vulcan salute.

Now wander off and do something else for a few minutes, and then test your anchor by repeating your gesture, creating your image or saying your word. Notice how this brings you back to your state of maximum resourcefulness.

If it doesn't seem quite right, then go back to the original experience, change something, set your anchor again, then test again. Do this as many times as you need, until you can call up your desired state at will – simply by using your anchor. Over time, your anchor will become so strong and streamlined that you won't even need to use it consciously.

Become used to testing things in this way as you go along. Officially, it's called the TOTE model[14], but I prefer to think of it as kids in the back of a car asking:

Are we there yet?

TOTE stands for:

T = test – to obtain feedback on how we're doing;

O = operate – intervene as necessary by changing something;

T = test again – to check if we've achieved the desired result. If not, we loop back to stage 2 (operate) and change something else.

E = exit – with the reassurance that we're on track.

It's essentially a self-correcting feedback loop. It presupposes that we've set ourselves a goal (a fixed outcome) that we can reach by any number of different routes (variable means). To check whether we're on the right track or not, we develop a test whereby we use our sensory acuity (noticing the effects of what we do, on ourselves and on others) to gather feedback. Based on that feedback, we either make an adjustment that will bring us nearer to our outcome or exit until the next time we need to check that we're still on course.

Chapter IV

Navigating our map of the world

This was one of the first concepts I learned in NLP. It's no exaggeration when I tell you that, in terms of turning my life around, it was probably the single most important thing I ever learned.

Our mental maps of the world are not the world. We can update our mental maps, especially our feelings and interpretations, more easily than we can change the world. What this means in practice is that people respond not to reality itself, but to their version of it. And that word *people* in the last sentence includes you and me, as well as everyone else.

For those of us who've been made redundant from a job, this is heady stuff. We've already started to understand how we can affect what goes on in our external experience by changing what happens on the inside. Now we can go deeper still and explore not just how we represent our map of the world to ourselves, but how others do the same.

Represent is an interesting word in this context. I could more accurately have typed it as *re-present* because that's exactly what we do. We *re-present* our external experience to ourselves using our five senses. If you doubt the truth of this, imagine eating a lemon and you'll start salivating.

In NLP, the five senses are called representational (rep) systems, usually abbreviated to VAKOG where:

V = visual (seeing)

A = auditory (hearing)

K = kinaesthetic (feeling)

O = olfactory (smelling)

G = gustatory (tasting).

We tend to favour one system over the others; this is known as our lead system. It shows up in our internal experience, our language and our physiology. Your lead system is the one that gives you immediate access to your memories. If you think of an event from your recent past, is it pictures (V), sounds (A) or feelings (K) that lead you back into the complete memory?

How you did that is a pretty reliable indicator of your dominant system, as is your language. Start noticing the type of vocabulary that you habitually use. Are you accustomed to:

keeping things in perspective; seeing your way forward (V);

keeping an ear to the ground; sounding people out (A);

rolling your sleeves up; getting to grips with an issue (K);

sniffing out a bargain; turning your nose up (O);

having exquisite taste; keeping everyone sweet (G)?

You probably think of a concert principally as an auditory experience. However, if three people with different leading rep systems enjoyed a musical evening, they would all remember and report their experience in very different ways:

- a visual person (V) might say:
  It was a beautiful concert; the hall was spectacular, and the music particularly colourful.

- an auditory person (A) could say:
  It was a resounding success; the hall had perfect acoustics, and the harmonies and chords rang out.

- a kinaesthetic person (K) might report:
  It was a moving concert; the hall was filled with emotion, and the music touched me deeply.

Bear in mind that these are only preferences. We all operate in all of the modes, depending on circumstances.

Physiology can also give us valuable clues as to how we and others process information internally. There's no such thing as a universal body language that's accurate 100% of the time, but our lead rep system does leave its mark on our body, in the same way as habitual gestures such as laughing, frowning and puzzling.

For now, just knowing what your lead system is can give you some really useful insights. It might even have shaped your career thus far. If you're a graphic or interior designer or work in the visual arts, science or engineering, it's odds-on that your visual preference is dominant. If you work with languages or music, your sensory preference will almost certainly be auditory. If you work with your hands as an osteopath, plasterer, medical practitioner or model-maker, then it's kinaesthetic. And imagine a career as a fragrance-blender or wine-taster without an olfactory or gustatory preference respectively.

If you stop and consider how you spend your leisure time, you'll probably discover that you follow your sensory preference here as well. Be aware of your strengths and weaknesses; this is information that could well be useful when we get to the second part of the book and start helping ourselves to find our new niche in life.

Our sensory strengths and weaknesses aren't set in stone though. In a very real sense, NLP is all about giving us more choice. One of those choices is over how we create our internal world. We may habitually favour one rep system over another, but that doesn't have to be our automatic default position.

If you're neglecting some of your rep systems, then set yourself the task of developing them. This can be great fun as well as enormously rewarding. Some of the people with whom I learned NLP decided they were going to develop their gustatory sense – by meeting once fortnightly to taste chocolate.

I spent my corporate career writing and producing publications so it's no surprise that my visual and auditory senses are well developed; my kinaesthetic wasn't though. I decided to change that. I started by hanging out with friend John who is profoundly kinaesthetic. I noticed how he did what he did. In his map of the world, going for a walk entails touching plants and trees, stroking dogs, and being aware of the texture and feel of seats and benches.

John was such a good role model that the tactile dimension of my surroundings is now very accessible to me. On a recent visit to an art gallery, nephew number three said to me:

I bet you're itching to touch that sculpture, aren't you?

I was.

I've spent some time explaining all of this because the mere fact of understanding that each of us has a map of the world that is unique to us and therefore completely different from anyone else's can bring about huge – and very positive – change in our life. A recent coaching session highlighted this very forcibly for me.

I was working with Petr, an executive who is highly intelligent and very successful, but who comes from a completely different culture. His culture is very much command and control, so it's OK for him to tell people at work to do something by a certain time, expect them to have done it, and give them a right royal rollicking if they haven't. Let's not bother with any of that namby-pamby stuff about finding out how they are, if they've understood the task, if they've got any questions.

Needless to say, this wasn't going down too well and was threatening to blight his career prospects. As Petr was about to start a new job in which he would have to manage teams, he was anxious to learn how to improve his people skills. It came as a complete and utter revelation to him that his map of the world was completely different from everyone else's.

Elaine: *Have you managed teams before?*

Petr: Yes.

Elaine: *How was it?*

Petr: *Well, people are either prepared to work or they're not. I don't care what's going on at home for them. I expect them to leave all that behind and concentrate on the task in hand.*

Elaine: *So how did people react to you?*

Petr: Some were OK; some weren't.

Elaine: *Have you ever thought that you could influence their response, that it might be rather like an action in physics where you provoke an equal and opposite reaction?*

Petr: *No.*

Elaine: *Want to learn how to do that?*

Petr: *Yes.*

-Time to do something.

At this point, I introduced Petr to what for me is the jewel in the crown of NLP. It's known as the meta-mirror. This is an amusing and enlightening little exercise that delivers powerful insights because it enables you to re-experience an event from four perspectives:

- first position – this is our own perspective; the I position. Knowing our own position helps us to get on in life and to develop ourselves.

- second position – this is the perspective of the other person; the you position. This involves understanding how someone else sees the world and appreciating their starting point. This enables us to develop empathy.

- third position – this is a neutral position; the they position. It involves stepping out of our own and the other person's perspective. It enables us to see the relationship from a more detached position.

- fourth position – this is the bonus position because it's the we perspective, the one in which, having been in all of the other three positions, we can identify with everyone involved in the interaction.

The best understanding comes from being able to operate out of all four positions.

There are three things you need to know about this exercise before you begin. One, you need to physically move into the different positions, so put pieces of paper or Post-It notes on the floor to help you:

4   **3**

2   **1**

Two, the first time you do it, it's probably best to pick an interaction with one other person where you would have wished for a better outcome. Three, it requires some imagination; just bear in mind that reality is an amazingly flexible concept and we make a lot of it up as we go along, so just go with the flow.

1	Stand in first position and imagine that you're looking at the other person in second position.	Notice your inner feelings, inner dialogue, body language, thoughts as you look at the other person.
	Break state by moving away from first position and thinking about something completely different such as what you ate for your last meal.	
2	Go and stand in the other person's position (second position), and look back at yourself in first position. As the other person, ask yourself:	What am I thinking and feeling about this person? What am I noticing about this person? How am I reacting to him/her?
	Break state by moving away from second position and thinking about something completely different such as the weather.	
3	Move to third position from where you can look back at the first two positions.	Consider both sides of the relationship from this impartial perspective. What do you notice about those two people over there? What do you observe about that you over there? How do you feel about that you in first position?
4	Move to fourth position, a place from where you can look back at first and third positions.	Look at that neutral you in third position and think about how you were. What resources did you have available? In your mind's eye, swap that you in the neutral third position back into the original you in first position.
5	Now go back to second position and stand in the other person's shoes again.	Notice how this is different; be aware of what's changed.
6	Finally come home to first position.	What do you notice? How does the relationship differ?

When Petr returned to first position for the last time, I noticed that he was leaning forwards – towards the other person. It was as if, having gained an understanding of that person's map of the world, he was prepared to stretch beyond his own and venture into the other person's.

Confirmation that this was indeed the case came a few days later. Petr had gone back to his home country and had met a friend who had a marked tendency to annoy him. Their meetings were usually relatively brief affairs; not this time though. They spent the whole day together, thoroughly enjoying one another's company. The next time I saw Petr, he asked:

What have you done to me?

The truth of the matter is that I hadn't done anything beyond giving Petr a passport to his own map of the world and a mirror that would reflect back to him what happens when his world collides with someone else's.

As my close friends will testify, I can be a tad slow on occasion. One of those occasions was my first encounter with my bête noire after he'd been the other person in my initial experience of the meta-mirror. I was walking down a corridor in the office at work, chatting to a colleague when I saw him approaching. He was a man of some consequence in the organization: on a bad day, he reduced me to an incoherent mess; on a good day, he reduced me to a slightly less incoherent mess.

I stopped talking in mid-sentence and my mouth probably went into that 'O' shape so beloved of cartoonists. Abandoning the conversation was rude, but my brain couldn't compute what was happening. I thought my eyesight had malfunctioned.

For me, this man had always been an ogre of gargantuan proportions, someone who dominated whatever space he was occupying, someone akin to Brian Blessed as Prince Vultan in the 1980 film of 'Flash Gordon'. Now, he'd metamorphosed into a small, short, grey-haired, middle-aged man with a vaguely disgruntled look on his face.

Oh, he's just a short man who feels uncomfortable in the presence of tall women. His problem; not mine.

We didn't exactly become best buddies, but we did end up with a respectful relationship that enabled us to work together and enjoy one another's sense of humour.

Speaking of humour, the funniest and most powerful example of the meta-mirror that I've come across was demonstrated by Maria, another coaching client who, in common with Petr, hails from a very different culture. She's also an alpha female of very decided views. We were doing the exercise in relation to a meeting with a subordinate that had been something of a disaster. Maria had just finished looking at the meeting from the first position for the final time.

Elaine: *So knowing what you now know, what would you do or say differently?*

Maria: *What do you mean?*

Elaine: *Well now that you've got the other person's perspective on the meeting, how would it be different?*

Maria: *It wouldn't.*

Elaine: (slightly puzzled) *Why not?*

Maria: *It wouldn't be different because it wouldn't have happened. I wouldn't be saying or doing anything because I wouldn't have called the meeting in the first place. How could I have been so lacking in judgement?*

Yes, well, I did say the insights could be powerful. In common with dogs, the meta-mirror is for life, not just for Christmas or any other past event that hasn't gone particularly well. You can use it to extremely good effect before events to model your own behaviour and the responses it evokes. In fact, you can use it whenever you want to get a different perspective on something.

Chapter V

Exploring our belief system

> ## PDJ
>
> *It is easier to change ourselves than to change others.*

No, I'm not the slightest bit interested in what you think makes the world go round. As we discovered in the previous chapter, we all have our own map of the world that works for us and enables us to operate out of whatever system of beliefs and values we choose to espouse.

What I am deeply interested in though is what we believe about ourselves. Why? Because what we believe about ourselves will be a determining influence not only on what we can do, but also on how we do it. As all the negative experiences of being made redundant that feature in this book demonstrate, sometimes the *how* can be just as important as the *what*.

I don't want you to get through life by coping with it; life's for living. I want you to be able to accomplish things with flair, flow, fluidity, flexibility, so let's get on with this belief thing.

We've already seen that our state can affect our behaviour, and our beliefs about ourselves fall into this same category. For example, if we believe ourselves to be redundant, as in the dictionary definition of:

no longer needed or useful; superfluous

then that is exactly how we'll start behaving. In my map of the world, redundancy applies to a job, not to an individual and certainly not to life, so you may want to reframe what you believe about your current status. At one point, I was:

fully employed discovering what I want to do next.

At another, I was:

working towards working.

Self-beliefs and states have something else in common as well. As a general rule, we're as ignorant about our self-beliefs as we are about our state. We usually simply run them in the background and never give them a second thought. Hold on a moment: are those alarm bells I can hear ringing? These beliefs have the power to affect the single most important relationship in our life: the one we have with ourselves.

Self-limiting beliefs fascinate me. We usually either impose them on ourselves or inherit them from authority figures in our childhood, then take them as gospel, and continue to be completely unaware of just how much they limit us.

In common with much else though, self-limiting beliefs don't have to be a permanent feature. Let's take an example. Larry Ellison is the co-founder of Oracle, the world's second largest software company. In childhood, his stepfather told him that he'd never amount to anything. Given that Mr Ellison now ranks as the third wealthiest American on the planet, I'd say that he amounts to quite a lot. I think we can safely assume that, even if he signed up to his stepfather's prediction for a while, he didn't allow it to become a self-limiting belief.

Many of us do though; we give authority figures from our past a degree of control over our beliefs about ourselves. Sometimes it's a surprisingly large degree, which was certainly the case with me. I was very tall very early, so I spent my childhood being the tallest girl in the class. Aged 12, I had a growth spurt and shot up still further with a commensurate increase in weight.

In the first gym class of the new academic year, Miss Dodgson, the gym mistress, weighed and measured us. Born in the 1920s, Miss Dodgson was firmly of the shape-up-or-ship-out-keep-your-emotions-under-control-there's-absolutely-no-reason-for-anyone-else-to-know-when-you're-having-your-period-girls school of discipline.

That September, she looks down at the scales and then sharply up at me.

Miss Dodgson: *Been on holiday?*

Elaine: (unnerved by this unusual conversational gambit) *Yes. Majorca.*

Miss Dodgson: *Well, eating that foreign food muck hasn't done you any good at all. You weigh a whopping eight stone. You're overweight.*

I'm devastated; I know how unhappy being overweight makes my mother. I don't want history to repeat itself. So I spend the next 40 years being overly concerned about my weight and thinking I'm fat. In spite of all the evidence to the contrary: the mirror, photographs, my own body, people's comments, I genuinely believe I have a weight problem.

It's only relatively recently that I've let go of this belief, prompted by some family photo albums that came to light when we were refurbishing our parental home. My parents had lovingly inscribed the date below each snap. I prepare to turn one particular page with trepidation:

This is it; we're coming to the point at which I put on all that weight.

I flip the page and see my 12-year old self standing in a corner of the garden. I'm wearing the dress I wore to my cousin's wedding. It's one of those Chinese tunic-style numbers with the stand-up collar. I'm the stick insect of popular myth; there isn't an ounce of fat on me.

I must have got the dates confused.

I continue turning the pages rapidly, desperate for the evidence that will prove I was overweight, that I've had a weight problem since my teens. There isn't any.

Wait a minute. I didn't even like Miss Dodgson; she humiliated me far too often on the hockey pitch, tennis court, rounders ground and parallel bars. Why have I allowed her to dominate my self-image for so long? What was I thinking?

After this minor outbreak of sanity, I conduct some research and realize that, if anything, at 5' 8" and eight stone I was actually underweight. But we're dealing with beliefs rather than facts here. I'd allowed a belief imposed on me by an authority figure to dictate that I could only ever wear baggy clothes, that my waist had to spend its life in hiding, that bikinis and I would remain strangers for ever, that I was somehow less worthy than my peers.

What's even more scary is that Miss Dodgson's dictum made it into my unconscious mind as well. For years, I had a recurring nightmare that I'd ended up in a beauty contest. I knew I wasn't meant to be there, but the moment was approaching when I'd have to squeeze my big, fat, ugly body into a skimpy swimsuit. Mercifully, I used to wake up at that point, grateful that I could hide my bodily inadequacies beneath the black shroud that used to do duty as my clothing.

It's something of a comfort to me to realize that I'm not the only person on the planet to have still been carrying a teacher's voice around in my head decades after leaving school. Leigh is another example. He's one of my redundancy coaching clients who is also dyslexic. When we started working together, his self-belief was so low as to be almost non-existent.

Leigh: *I'll never get another job. I'm stupid.*

Elaine: *How do you know?*

Leigh: *What?*

Elaine: *How do you know you're stupid?*

Leigh: *Because that was the message my teachers gave me – every day for ten years.*

Elaine: *Do you still believe everything your teachers told you?*

Leigh: *Not sure; never really given it much thought.*

Elaine: *But you do believe that you're stupid, just because your teachers said you were?*

Leigh: *It sounds silly when you put it like that, but why would I not believe them?*

Elaine: *Where's the evidence to the contrary, the evidence that proves you're bright, clever, intelligent?*

With a certain amount of prompting, Leigh came to realize that lack of academic success doesn't equal stupidity. He managed to find plenty of examples in both his working and social life when he'd been the one to solve problems, find a way forward, get things moving – even though he'd been surrounded by people with all kinds of academic qualifications.

By the time that session ended, Leigh had found lots of internal validation – from his own experience – that he was intelligent in a different way, but I sensed that he needed some external validation as well. So I sent him a link to an IQ test; I deliberately didn't put any pressure on him to take it. I made it clear that the choice was his. Both of us were taking a risk. If the results confirmed his teachers' assessment, I would have left him in a worse place than I found him: a complete no-no for any coach and an absolute disaster for Leigh's self-esteem.

The day he phoned me with the results was one of the highlights of my coaching career to date. He was almost incoherent with excitement. The results had highlighted the things at which Leigh truly excelled: communicating, problem-solving, taking different perspectives. They'd also confirmed in an objective and reliable way that Leigh's IQ was higher than average, so high in fact that his test score surpassed that of most of his friends who'd been through higher education.

In the NLP map of the world, self-limiting beliefs fall into three categories:

- hopelessness – I can't achieve my goal under any circumstances.

- helplessness – I don't have the ability to achieve my goal.

- worthlessness – I don't deserve my goal because of something I am/am not or something I've done/haven't done.

Let's bring our self-limiting beliefs out into the limelight and see what we've got. This is the first step to overcoming them. Think about it for a moment: what are your self-limiting beliefs keeping out of your life in this transitional phase? Your beliefs won't like being questioned, but we're going to do it anyway – for one simple reason. They won't stand up to close scrutiny.

- If you're feeling hopeless, ask yourself:
  why can't I achieve my goal?

- If you're feeling helpless, ask yourself:
  what abilities don't I have?

- If you're feeling worthless, ask yourself:
  why don't I deserve to have my goal?

Be aware that beliefs are herd animals at heart and tend to pop up in clusters. Just keep on calmly analyzing them one by one as they appear. Once you understand how a belief serves your best interests, albeit at the cost of some undesirable side effects, you can think about replacing it.

Leigh came to understand that he'd been feeding off a toxic combination of hopelessness, helplessness, and worthlessness.

My dyslexia had become my excuse for everything. I didn't deserve to have anything because I had it. I couldn't achieve anything because I had it. I didn't even need to try any more because I had it.

When we stripped Leigh's beliefs right back, we discovered that his dyslexia had become part of his identity. For as long as this was the case, it was impossible for him to tackle his poisonous educational inheritance. Once he realized that he could still be himself without dyslexia playing quite such a prominent part in his life, he began to experience life very differently.

Julia, another of my coaching clients, used to believe that she didn't deserve (worthlessness) to be alive because she was outliving her mother who had died when relatively young. The positive intent of this belief for Julia was to honour her mother; its side effects were a miserable and unfulfilled life.

The day that Julia understood that she could honour her mother by doing all those things in her own lifetime that were denied to her mother (having a successful career; seeing her children reach adulthood; becoming a grandmother) was the day that transformed her life.

Chapter VI

Minding our Ps and Qs

> ## PDJ
>
> *We cannot not communicate.*
>
> *We communicate continuously in all three major*
>
> *rep systems: visual, auditory and kinaesthetic.*

Maybe it's because I'm a copywriter as well as a coach, but language looms really large in both my daily existence and my coaching practice. In this chapter, I shall be talking about language in its broadest sense of how we communicate with ourselves internally and others externally.

Regardless of whether our relationship with ourselves is healthy and positive or unhealthy and negative, we typically communicate with ourselves by making pictures, hearing voices and experiencing feelings. What we're doing here is representing our experience to ourselves using the rep systems we learned about in chapter IV. Cue to learn a smidgeon more. Could the submodalities please enter stage left?

Without getting too technical, submodalities are the building blocks of the rep systems. Examples of visual submodalities are size of the picture, brightness, still or moving, black and white or colour. Auditory submodalities include volume, speed, tone, distance; kinaesthetic ones range from location and pressure to temperature and rhythm.

An example will undoubtedly make this easier to understand, so let's start with the pictures. I was working with Helen, a client who had a somewhat troubled relationship with her teenage daughter. A difficult conversation between the two was looming, and Helen wanted to go through it mentally ahead of time to get some idea of how it might play out. Excellent idea, except she couldn't get started because she had such a huge, bright, upsetting picture of her last interaction with her daughter in her visual field.

Elaine: *So this picture that's upsetting you is big and bright and in the way?*

Helen: *Uhuh.*

Elaine: *I'm assuming it's in colour, so make all the colour drain out of it until it's black and white. Then experiment with making it smaller and pushing it further away.*

Helen: *OK, I've done that.*

Elaine: *Is the picture still bothering you?*

Helen: *Of course not; it's way off over there. I can hardly see it.*

In Helen's case, the submodality that made the most difference was distance, but it varies from person to person. This is one of those things that you can only find out about yourself by experimenting and noticing what happens, but that's just another excuse to be playful, so be prepared to play.

Moving on to the voices, the first thing to acknowledge is that we all talk to ourselves on the inside. It's perfectly normal, unless you begin to vocalize it in the presence of others, at which point you will notice people giving you sidelong glances and edging discreetly away from you.

Let's assume that we all know how to keep our inner dialogue to ourselves and let's examine how we say what we say. Is our tone friendly, forgiving, sympathetic, encouraging? Or is at the other extreme: harsh and critical? If it's in the latter category, just stop and think about it. We're treating ourselves with extreme disrespect. How would we feel if a third party treated us in that way?

The tone we use gives us a very clear indication of the state of our relationship with ourselves. Secondly, if we do talk to ourselves in that manner, whose voice is it? As Miss Dodgson demonstrated so clearly, it may very well not be our own, but could belong to a parent, teacher, or former boss perhaps.

Let's revert back to Leigh, my dyslexic client, for a moment. He'd already started to feel better about himself and his abilities, but he still had the critical voices in his head. I used submodalities with Leigh and his voices in much the same way as I had with Helen and her pictures.

I asked Leigh to take himself back to school and briefly relive an experience when a teacher was being critical, paying particular attention to the voice. Then I asked him to experiment with the voice by slowing it down, speeding it up, pushing it further away, making it sound like his favourite cartoon character – and to notice how his emotional response to it changed, even though the words remained the same.

When Leigh had discovered the exact combination of auditory submodalities that took the power away from the voice, I asked him to imagine that he had a set of controls in his head that he could use to turn down the volume very gradually until the voice no longer existed.

I don't remember working with a kinaesthetic client using submodalities, so I was stuck for an example to use here until serendipity intervened – as it seems to do so often these days. I'm reading a children's book called 'Head Games' by Mariah Fredericks. It's all about computer gaming and what happens when reality and fantasy collide.

It's so different from the sort of stuff I usually read that the mere fact that I've borrowed it from the library is an example of behavioural flexibility which we'll come onto in chapter VIII.

Here's some text from chapter ten:

A test. My stomach clenches. A voice in my head. This is it, the reason you shouldn't have come…

…I have a weird, floaty feeling in my stomach, and my fingers are all numb. That's probably my body telling me this whole situation is bad news. I take a deep breath to get rid of the floaty feeling.[16]

What this text demonstrates is that Judith Ellis, the 15-year-old heroine, has a primary kinaesthetic rep system which leads her into internal dialogue with herself. Once she's interpreted the meaning of her feelings using her auditory rep system, she reverts to kinaesthetic and changes something in that system: her breath.

Before we move on to the external world, I'd just like to draw your attention to one other mode of internal communication: our way of being, commonly known as association and dissociation. I've already referred to this briefly when I was talking about anchors.

If you're associated into your own experience, you're looking out at the world from your own eyes. If you're dissociated, you're seeing yourself at one remove, rather as though you're looking at yourself on a projector screen. Take a moment to work out whether you favour one over the other or whether you switch between the two.

Both have their pluses and minuses: association means you experience everything to the full; dissociation enables you to view events from a distance, thereby gaining perspective. However, there are occasions when both of them can be the wrong tool for the job.

If you associate into both positive and negative events, you'll feel amazing and awful in equal measure, but you won't learn anything from the negatives because you don't know how to step back and view the event from a different standpoint.

If you dissociate from both types of event, you're not really engaged with any single aspect of your own life, although you could give a master class in analyzing your own experience from a distance.

If you associate into the negative and dissociate from the positive, you're unwittingly signing up to wretchedness. You're not only making the most of whatever unhappiness comes your way, you're also completely oblivious not only to feeling good about the good things in your life, but also to the daily presence of such things.

If you do the opposite and associate into the positive and dissociate from the negative, you've found the holy grail. You'll notice the positive things in your life and feel good about them, but will also be able to step back, re-examine negative experiences in a different light, and learn from them.

As with much else, this is something that we can control – just by monitoring whether we're viewing the exterior world from inside or outside our own body. Speaking as a reformed hard-core dissociator, I can put my hand on my heart and testify to the scale of the difference that this can make in daily experience.

Now let's turn our attention to our external communication. We'll use as an example a negative life experience that's going to be positively unhelpful to you as you get over redundancy.

Let's imagine you've had a particularly unsatisfactory job interview where you didn't come away with a new job, but you did come away with negative feelings about how you perform in interviews. That's certainly not going to help when you go for your next interview, so let's see what we can do about it in advance.

Here's how it panned out with one of my clients who was dreading a upcoming interview because of a previous bad experience.

Sally: *I'll cock the interview up. I know I will; it's always the same with me.*

Elaine: (with quizzical eyebrow and tone) *You've always cocked interviews up? In every single one you've ever experienced, stretching right back to childhood?*

Sally: (indignantly) *No, of course not. Don't be daft. I've actually done quite well in some. I got into a very good secondary school when there were 20 children after each place, I got the much sought after lead role in an am-dram production last year, and I got my previous job.*

Elaine: *So how are you feeling about your interview now?*

Sally: *Differently.*

Elaine: *Great word. What's the difference that makes the difference between your good interview experiences and the bad one?*

Sally: *Well, now that I think about it, those three interviews had a lot in common. There'd been loads of preliminary stuff to get through. I was feeling really confident because I'd done so well in that. I had a sense of 'If you still don't want me, it's your loss'. And I remember that I prepared myself physically as well as mentally. I stood outside the door, took three calming breaths, said to myself 'Sally, you're on', and went in.*

Elaine: *Is that similar to what you do when you go on stage in your am-dram productions?*

Sally: *Similar? It's identical. How could I have been so bloody stupid? It's just another type of performance.*

I realize that not all of us are accomplished actors, but there's still a lot that we can learn from Sally's experience. Her starting point is particularly interesting because it includes that word *always*.

This belongs to a group of words and expressions known as universal quantifiers which essentially means that they hold true on every single occasion or set of circumstances; absolutely no exceptions allowed. I shall be referring to them less formally as universals. Familiarity born of years gives me this right: at one point, my life was infested with them. Not a good place to be; enough said.

Examples of other universals are *never, nobody, none, no, nowhere, nothing, no-one, ever, every, everyone, everywhere, everybody, everything, always, anything, all* and *each*. They can also be much less obvious, as in:

Dogs smell horrible.

What? All dogs? Everywhere? There's never been a single example of a fragrant dog ever since the world began?

If you look back at Sally's first utterance, you'll realize that she couldn't have expressed that thought (*it's always the same with me*) without the universal. In the previous chapter, Leigh did exactly the same:

I'll never get another job.

One of the things I find particularly amusing is that we frequently tell our children not to be so silly when they come rushing home from school with sentiments such as:

Nobody likes me.

I'll never be able to read.

The other boys always pick on me.

When we apply universals to ourselves though, we often fail to pick up on them:

No-one will ever give me a job.

I always look and sound dreadful in interviews.

Everything I've ever done is irrelevant for this position.

You'll notice that I challenged Sally's use of the universal by taking it to such an extreme that it prompted her to search through her experience until she found some counter-examples. This is something that you can do for yourself. Now that you know what *universals* are, listen out for them and challenge your own thinking.

You may remember that finding the difference that makes the difference is where NLP started. Using this technique makes you aware of subtle distinctions between experiences that are all labelled with the same descriptor: interview, in this case. Until I asked that question, Sally didn't have a clue what the difference was between her successful and unsuccessful interviews.

Once she had that information, she had her own formula for success. She knew what she needed to do to be at her best for her forthcoming interview. In Sally's case, answering the question led her to compare and contrast her different interview experiences. This can be a really helpful thing to do. As soon as Sally realized that an interview was nothing more than another performance, much of her uneasiness dissipated because she was back in familiar territory.

Time for some more new linguistic friends: modal operators of necessity. What?! I know: they sound hideously complicated, but you'll recognize them when you hear them. And, in future, when you do hear them, I want you to promise to challenge them. They're words such as *should, shouldn't, must, mustn't, ought, oughtn't, have to.*

I must spend three hours today cleaning and polishing the car until I can see my own reflection in the bodywork.

Really? Who says so? What would happen if you didn't?

There are, of course, numerous occasions in our life when we do have to fulfil certain responsibilities both to ourselves and to others. What we're talking about here is the nature of the relationship we have with ourselves and the manner in which we do things. If we regard something as a chore, a necessary evil in our life, then that's exactly what it will be.

We all too often imagine that we have someone standing over us with a whip commanding us to do this, that or the other. I think what's driving us here is competitiveness.

Having been the product of two ultra-competitive schools, I tend to the view that competitiveness is somewhat over-rated. That may, of course, simply be a function of the fact that I was very rarely top of anything. Even so, these days, daily life can be intensely competitive. Let's remember though that we do have a choice over the extent to which we engage with that competitiveness. Do we really have to be the fittest person in the gym or the best dressed person at the school gates?

Personally, I've experienced a huge sense of liberation since I've let go of the idea that I have to excel at everything. As a dyspraxic person, I'm probably the largest blot on the landscape ever to have entered the gym in the eyes of my aerobics and Zumba teachers. I regularly find myself (and see myself, thanks to those wretched mirrors) facing in a different direction from everyone else, lifting the wrong limb in the wrong rhythm, and being at least one pace behind. But hey, I'm exercising and having a good time, so does it matter?

We can also cut ourselves some slack. Compassion seems to be on the edge of extinction; self-compassion – even as a concept, let alone a daily habit – seems to have already toppled over the edge. Marcus, one of my corporate coaching clients, had absolutely no idea what I was talking about when I introduced him to self-compassion.

Marcus: *Is that the same as I when I buy myself a Mars bar?*

Elaine: *No, Marcus, that's called giving yourself a little treat which is also a great thing to do. Self-compassion is all about accepting that you're a human being, that you're liable to make mistakes. Instead of beating yourself up when you put a foot wrong, get into the habit of forgiving yourself and seeing what you can learn from your mistake. That way, you'll take the learning with you the next time you're in a similar situation.*

I didn't hear from Marcus for a considerable time after that session, so I phoned him up just to check that he was OK. He was so OK that he ceased to be a client; learning the art of self-compassion was all he needed to do.

Chapter VII

Mining our own resources

> ## PDJ
>
> *We already either have all the resources we need to achieve our desired outcome or we can create them.*

Resources are a really important concept in NLP and an incredibly valuable tool in our daily life. They can best be defined as anything that can help us to achieve our desired outcome, to move us from where we are currently to where we want to be.

They can include our state, our beliefs, our memories, our physiology, our experiences, as well as people, places, possessions, stories and events. This list is by no means exhaustive; one man's resource can be another man's obstacle, to paraphrase very, very loosely.

One of the most amazing features of searching for and finding resources is that you can use a time machine to do it. You can identify a resource that you had when you were younger but have now lost (generally because of external – and often misplaced – pressure to *grow out of it*) and bring it into your present.

You can take a resource that you possess now and take it back to help your younger self. This makes use of that wonderful ability known as hindsight which sometimes gets a bad press. Not in this context, it doesn't. Things that you know now but didn't at an earlier stage in your life count as resources big time.

You can even go into the future, imagine that you've already solved an issue using a particular resource, and then bring that resource back to either your current or younger self.

Another great thing about resources is that they're the flirts of the NLP world: they'll hang out with anyone, anywhere, any time at all. Just think The Jackson 5 or Mariah Carey, depending on age:

Just call my name and I'll be there.

Ryan, a 20-year-old dyslexic client who was taking his 'A' Levels for the fourth time, was outstandingly good at mining his own resources. He was studying science and maths and needed to remember a bewildering number of complicated formulae for his exams. He found this exceptionally difficult.

However, Ryan and I soon discovered that he had a very creative visual memory – as is often the case with dyslexics – so he used this as a resource. He drew the formulae and created a story around them. In no time at all, we were surrounded by representations of comic characters who did and didn't want to bond with one another.

Ryan had a couple of other exam-related issues:

Ryan: *I find those big blocks of text really intimidating, really difficult to read. Even when I get to the end, I'm not sure that I've understood everything properly.*

Elaine: *What would help with that?*

Ryan: *I know I go too fast, so I need to slow myself down.*

I hope I never forget this next part. His mum had left us with some Maynards' Wine Gums. Ryan picked out a red, yellow, and green gum and designed himself a traffic light. Then he practised by visualizing an imaginary traffic light at the end of every sentence, and only turning the light to green once he was sure he'd understood.

On to the next issue:

Ryan: *I can't stop answering a question once I've started it.*

Elaine: *Even if you think you're not going to get good marks for it?*

Ryan: *Even when I know I haven't got a scoobie.*

Elaine: *So think of a time when you have been able to stop yourself doing something.*

Ryan: *When I was much younger, I stopped myself from laughing out loud at funerals and stuff like that because I'd have got into trouble with the adults if I hadn't.*

Elaine: *How did you do that?*

Ryan: *I made up this little character in my head. He was like a super-hero. He had the power to make me do anything he wanted.*

Elaine: *Think he could help you to move onto the next exam question?*

Ryan: *Yes, he's still there in my head; just hasn't been around much recently.*

I rather suspect that little character was around more often during exam time, given that Ryan is now at university studying to be a mining engineer. I'll refrain from the mining resources/mining engineer pun.

What Ryan demonstrates par excellence is that resources are both eminently transferable and always up for a spot of comparing and contrasting. For instance, if making presentations gives you the collywobbles, ask your unconscious mind to think of a similar situation that's collywobbles-free.

Raj is a good example of this; he's an ambitious and testosterone-fuelled young man who is preparing for his promotion board.

Raj: *I'm terrified of boards, panels, all that interview stuff.*

Elaine: *What is there in your life that's similar but doesn't terrify you?*

Raj: *I love public speaking; have done since grammar school. I've won lots of competitions and I still make presentations at professional meetings.*

Elaine: *And what is there about public speaking that could help you in interviews?*

Raj: *It's essentially the same activity isn't it? The only thing that's different is the scale. In both cases, I'm talking to a group of people and, when people ask me questions at the end, it's even more similar because then it's one-on-one and I'm having to think on my feet.*

I only asked Raj two questions and he did the rest. What's interesting about the questions though is that they're both based on the positive presupposition that something a) similar and b) helpful already existed in his life. I deliberately excluded a negative response.

This can be a useful technique when you're challenging yourself. And by now you're getting into the swing of challenging yourself, what with looking out for universals, modal operators of necessity, self-limiting beliefs and association/dissociation.

The next thing to understand about resources is that, even if they habitually hang out with someone else, you can still call them over and they're all yours – which brings us neatly onto role modelling. I've already mentioned this briefly; this is where I get serious about it.

As usual, there's an NLP presupposition:

Modelling excellence leads to excellence.

Understanding the mechanics of your role models' behaviour will give you the key to how they do what they do. This can often be hugely entertaining.

As part of my coaching training, I had to learn a new skill of my choice by modelling someone who had it. I think most other people picked something heavyweight and worthy; me, I decided to learn how to flirt. Adolescence passed me by somehow so I'd never learned this fascinating skill. I had two models: a delightful Portuguese woman on the coaching course and a gay friend. They gave me a master class in the art and science of flirting. Now, I can't imagine life without it.

If you become curious about other people's behaviour, you'll automatically start noticing how they do what they do best. You may even want to ask them some very specific questions. However, you can also indulge in unconscious modelling – just by hanging out with your role models. If you build enough rapport with them and have enough imagination to put yourself in their place, you'll begin to get a glimpse of how they experience the world.

This is how we learn as young children. You've probably already picked up on the fact that I think they're the best role models of all: willing to give anything a go, endlessly resourceful, and with absolutely no fear of failure.

I can hear a technique creeping up on us. It's been a while; this one goes by the name of circle of excellence. Its use is confined strictly to those occasions when you want to move from your present state to your desired state.

1   Sketch out an imaginary circle on the floor.

2   Think of a challenging situation in your near future.

3   Ask yourself: What resources will I need? Pay particular attention to your language and the labels that you give each resource. You're looking for three resources.

4   Ask your subconscious to identify occasions when you've had those resources. Just notice what floats to the forefront of your mind.

5   Now step into your circle on the floor and relive the experience associated with the first resource. Say softly to yourself: See what I see, hear what I hear, and feel what I feel.

6   Use an image, word or discreet gesture to anchor the resource.

7   Step out of your circle and break state by thinking about something mundane.

8   Repeat steps 5, 6 and 7 for the next two resources.

9   Step back into the circle and use your anchor to re-access all of these resources. See the challenging situation, take your resources into it, and notice what's different.

10 If you need another resource, repeat steps 3 to 9 until you feel completely congruent.

11 Imagine yourself in that future situation and see, hear and feel how you will be different with these new resources.

Just so you know, step 11 goes by the name of future pacing. It's a way both of testing that the resources we've created are transferable to the outside world and of anchoring those resources to the specific situations in which they're going to be most useful.

Let's finish this chapter with one of the four pillars of NLP: sensory acuity. At the very beginning of this book, I defined it as:

noticing the effects of what you do, on yourself and others.

What I'm suggesting here is that you get into the habit of using your sensory acuity to notice what you're doing well each day. It's a particularly important practice in the context of acknowledging your own resources because it enables you to gather feedback about yourself and to give yourself credit where credit's due.

I remember once describing this strategy to a work colleague and she immediately told me that she'd never done anything of which she was proud. What not one single solitary thing in her 40+ years on the planet? Time for a reframe. We do not have to have written a blockbuster before breakfast, broken the land speed record before lunch, and learned three languages during our evening commute.

What we do have to do is train ourselves to be aware of our own behaviour, particularly when we're doing something fluently and naturally, and achieving the outcome that we want. It's a sad reflection on daily life that failure tends to receive more attention than success. Just pick up a paper, or watch a news bulletin.

Try this instead. Now this may make you laugh, but I swear that I've been doing it since 2004 – way before British comedienne Miranda Hart erupted onto our television screens in 'Miranda'. Before you go to sleep, cast your mind back over your day and pick out five things that have made you proud of yourself.

Yes, it has huge echoes of Heather Small and of Miranda in her joke shop and if that makes you laugh, then that's just an added bonus. My experience has been that it makes me feel good about myself, builds my self-esteem, and is a very positive way to end the day. See what it does for you.

Chapter VIII

Finding our flexibility

> ## PDJ
>
> *Having choice is better than not having choice.*

Readers of a certain age will remember a credit card called Access. Its mission was to rival the already well-established Barclaycard. It failed and consequently disappeared from our wallets. During its relatively brief lifespan, it was known as *our flexible friend* and appeared in a series of adverts as an unendingly bendable green and red card with facial features. That's what we're going for: the unendingly bendable; not the green and red – that's entirely optional.

You'll remember that at the start of this book, I defined behavioural flexibility as:

realizing that we always have more than one choice.

In the context of redundancy, we can also regard it as the practice of doing things that we wouldn't normally do, of acting outside our comfort zone. I believe this is a particularly valuable skill to develop when you're in transition because it enables you to do something different when what you usually or currently do isn't working.

It opens up new perspectives for you. For example, if you've already applied for more than 50 jobs on-line and haven't received a single acknowledgement, let alone an interview, then that could be the trigger for asking yourself:

What would happen if I did something different here?

You'll have gathered by now that I'm massively in favour of being playful. In my map of the world, behavioural flexibility is a practice that invites playfulness. You can almost start doing it as a game, and then be pleasantly surprised at what happens.

When I was learning NLP, I experimented with behavioural flexibility when some semi-unwelcome guests turned up for a meal at mine. Instead of greeting them unenthusiastically, I opened my arms in welcome. They responded in kind, and that initial warm exchange somehow permeated the rest of the proceedings. An event that I'd been dreading, that I thought I'd have to get through the best I could, became a thoroughly enjoyable experience.

The great thing about behavioural flexibility is that it's like a muscle that you can strengthen. And you don't have to spend hours working out in a gym to do it. Using NLP is much like being at the (sadly defunct) Woolworths' pick 'n' mix sweeties counter. You can mix and match as many of these as you fancy without any fear of going wrong.

Vary your routine
This is probably a good place to start. Deconstruct your daily routine and do things differently. Read a different newspaper or magazine, listen to a different radio station, watch a television programme you wouldn't normally dream of watching, take a different route to the shops, brush your teeth using your non-dominant hand. Research by

Case Western Reserve University[17] shows that this last activity can both increase your mental flexibility and improve your stamina for completing tasks. As a bonus, it will also even up the wear on your teeth on both sides.

Practise random acts of kindness

These are another good way of building behavioural flexibility. The concept and practice of performing selfless acts for others has probably existed for centuries, but such acts seem to have entered the popular consciousness in the 1980s. Since then, they've been sponsored by various radio and television shows, featured in films and fiction, and been the subject of two books by humorist Danny Wallace.[18]

You can design your own acts – from the proverbial helping the old lady across the road to letting shoppers in front of you in the supermarket queue – and most of them cost absolutely no money. You do get paid though. When you do something unexpected for someone that you don't know and with no prospect of gain, you receive a lovely little thrill on the inside and a smile from the other person on the outside.

Researchers at Bangor University may have calculated that the monetary value of a smile is one-third of a penny[19], but I'm with the popular saying that:

You can't put a price on a smile.

When someone genuinely smiles at you with laugh lines in the corner of their eyes, you respond in kind and your mood lifts. That's the funny thing about random acts of kindness: they make the giver feel just as good – maybe even better – than the recipient. As The Book says:

It is more blessed to give than to receive.[20]

Such acts won't, of course, always meet with a positive reaction. Some years ago, my recently retired father was in the first flush of enthusiasm for giving something back to the community. While walking down the hill to the shops, he passed a decrepit house with an equally unkempt old gentleman leaning over the gate. My father – an accomplished DIYer – decided to offer his services to the man and his house.

I just wish you and all the other f***ers who want to keep interfering in my f***ing life would just f*** off and leave me alone.

If you're a tad sensitive about rejection, you can use these experiences to explore the why, what and how of that particular emotion. That too will lead to more flexibility.

On other occasions, you'll have to work hard to convince people that you're acting out of genuine altruism. They just can't believe that you're for real; in their map of the world, there must be an ulterior motive lurking around somewhere.

I once warned a fellow driver about an inconspicuous parking bay suspension notice. I didn't want him to make the same mistake I'd made the previous week: park in the bay unwittingly and have to pay the hefty fine. Even after I'd marched him up to the notice and pointed it out to him, he still regarded me with suspicion, convinced it was some kind of scam.

Why on earth would you do that for me?

I persisted; here was an additional opportunity to extend my behavioural flexibility – by practising my skills of persuasion. Eventually, the driver realized I was on the level, thanked me, and smiled. I smiled in return. Job done: behavioural flexibility extended.

Get into the as if frame

This is another fabulous little technique for developing your behavioural flexibility so that it resembles Popeye's legendary biceps. This is simplicity itself; all it requires is that we act as if something is other than it is. Often we don't do it because it doesn't occur to us. We're stuck so firmly in the here and now, in the what is – with all its problems and obstacles, that we forget to engage our imagination.

One of my corporate coaching clients demonstrated this as if ability par excellence recently. She was responsible for convincing some very senior colleagues that they could run a pilot workshop, even though they were way behind schedule.

As she entered the meeting room, the atmosphere reeked of twisted knickers and hot air. Everyone rushed to tell her why the workshop was an impossibility in the time available.

Why don't we just put all that to one side and talk about it as if it were possible?

Two hours later, everyone left the meeting knowing exactly what they had to do to make the workshop happen on the appointed day. The magic of the as if frame had transformed it from an impossibility into a reality.

Get curious about other people

Curiosity seems to be out of favour these days. It's probably all to do with respecting privacy, gagging orders, data protection and curiosity's close kinship with nosiness. It can, however, be a valuable ability to develop, particularly if you begin to get curious about other people and how they do what they do.

If you're in the middle of an unpleasant interaction with someone and you become curious about their behaviour, this automatically distances you from the interaction, thereby changing your relationship to it. Curiosity will also stop you going into auto-pilot and reacting the way you habitually react in such situations. There's an important lesson here: reactivity is the opposite of flexibility. The first triggers an automatic response; the second enables you to choose your response.

The best example I can think of dates from my pre-NLP days so it doesn't reflect well on me, but I'll share it with you anyway. I was driving down the middle lane of the M3 in the morning rush-hour on my way to work. A car cut in front of me so sharply that the driver offended my sense of territorial imperative. I went straight into road rage mode: flashing lights, hooting horn, frantic facial and arm gestures, the full works.

Instead of reacting in kind, the other driver looked into his rear view mirror, made eye contact with me, and started hitting himself over the head in Monty Pythonesque mode. My anger dissipated instantly; I was helpless with laughter. One simple gesture conveyed so much:

I'm sorry: that was an idiotic thing to do, but I'm only human. Please forgive me.

It also broke the pattern of action and reaction that could have led to us engaging in automotive combat until one of us turned off the motorway. More importantly, it made me curious – not just about the other driver's behaviour, but also about my own.

Take up role-modelling
We've discussed this in the previous chapter, so don't need to dwell on it for too long here. If you want to expand your behavioural flexibility

to include a skill that you don't currently possess, step number one is to find yourself someone who does. Apart from anything else, acquiring a new skill will do wonders for your self-confidence, so what have you got to lose?

I shall just reiterate here that role models don't have to be human or even exist in the real world. You can pick an animal or a character from a book or a film. I once whiled away a slow-moving rush-hour bus journey by modelling a puppy who'd got on the bus with his owner. I soon realized that, for our canine companions, smell is the most important sense. I gradually became aware of the range of odours confined in that relatively small space. Sadly, not all of them were an undiluted pleasure for my heightened olfactory senses.

Maybe not knowing quite what you're going to get with role models is all part of their charm.

Adopt a different perspective

We've already seen how well this one works in chapter IV when we were having fun with the meta-mirror. Get into the habit of looking at things from other people's perspectives and notice what your unconscious mind serves up to you. Use some of your role models from above. How would they react in your situation? I'm often amazed at the rapidity with which this works.

Last summer, I reprimanded my neighbour for parking his people carrier across my drive. He took exception to my tone. Even though I apologized, the air bristled with tension as he stormed back into his house, slamming the front door behind him. The next time I saw my neighbour he was outside that same front door surrounded by numerous family members. I hate confrontation so my natural instinct was to hide, but I knew he'd already seen me and I had to walk past his house to reach mine. I could feel the panic rising, so I asked myself:

What would my father have done?

My body knew before my mind did. I could feel myself expanding into the hail-fellow-well-met mixed with a modicum of devil-may-care attitude so natural to my father. The behaviour followed the physiology: I smiled and wished my neighbour and his family a hearty *good morning* as I passed – and elicited a similar response from them. Being able to make that simple gesture just felt so good. Without it, I'm pretty sure we'd have been deep into not speaking territory.

Chuck out those self-limiting beliefs

We've already discussed these in chapter V, so I'm going to do something that I don't normally do (behavioural flexibility at large) and make an assumption. I'm assuming that you were paying attention and that you're now permanently on the look-out for the universals and modal operators of necessity in your life.

All I shall be doing here is making three requests.

1 If you hear yourself using a universal of any stripe whatsoever, challenge it so vigorously that you find at least two counter-examples.

2 If you hear yourself saying:
   I shouldn't/mustn't/can't do whatever,

   ask yourself:
   What's stopping me?

3 If you hear yourself saying:
   I should/ought to/must do whatever.

   ask yourself:
   What would happen if I didn't?

Do you think we should take him out of his comfort zone?

Get yourself out of that comfort zone

Comfort zones have a lot going for them. We've already discussed how useful they can be as a safe haven in times of transition. There's much to be said though for expanding their frontiers, particularly if you're on a mission to build behavioural flexibility. One of NLP's presuppositions is that:

If you do what you've always done, you'll get what you've always got.

An easy way of getting something different is to deliberately put yourself in new situations. You won't be able to either revert to type or default to auto-pilot because you won't have been in this situation before.

I'm not necessarily talking about anything major here; it all depends on the size of your comfort zone. For me, at one point in my life, chatting to people in the queue at the supermarket would have been a stretch. Now, I'll talk to anyone anywhere – and usually do. That's the outcome we want: a discernible change in your behaviour, in the number and type of situations in which you feel at ease.

Chapter IX

Taking a trip down our timeline

PDJ

We make the best choice available to us at the time, but many more choices of which we are unaware usually also exist.

The unfortunate fact that our employers have made us redundant from a job does not make us, as individuals, redundant. We may, however, not be as complete as we were when we had a job.

Did you throw something of yourself away when you dumped your business cards? If you've left any part of your identity with your former employer, then you need to go back and retrieve it. And no; I'm not going to subject you to the humiliating experience of passing through the corporate portals again.

Welcome to timelines – yet another really useful NLP concept. Understanding our relationship to time is an essential part of understanding ourselves. We collect memories of our decisions, our experiences – both good and bad – over time. How we store those memories affects how we experience life.

We can't change what's happened to us – redundancy, in this case, but we can change how we store the memory of that event. For me, this is akin to changing the machine code of a computer. Machine code is the lowest level of software; it tells the computer what to do. What we're doing here is telling our brains what to do when we recall the memory of redundancy.

Before we start experimenting with timelines, I'll just bring you up to date on the basics. We all represent time to ourselves in our own way. To find out how you do it, ask yourself:

Where's my past? Where's my future?

Use your arms to point in the appropriate direction. I've been on training courses where people have practically but unintentionally poked other people's eyes out during this exercise because of where their hands have landed.

If you flung one arm in front of you and the other behind, then you're in the timeline pattern known as *in time*. If you spread your arms wide, then you're using the pattern known as *through time.* Each pattern will affect not only how we perceive time, but also how we establish our priorities and conduct our life.

The crucial difference between the two patterns is that *in time* people have their timeline passing through their body while *through time* people have their timeline somewhere in front of them. Although timelines generally conform to one of these two basic orientations of front/back and left/right, there can be enormous variations within that. The lines can be curved, in steps, spirals or loops; they can even be three-dimensional or dynamic.

In time individuals can be so associated into their experiences, so in the here and now, that they lose track of time and can be late for meetings. They may avoid any form of planning or deadline-setting, and can find it difficult to compare events because they store their memories in sequence.

Through time individuals, on the other hand, can be somewhat dissociated from their own experience. They have a very keen awareness of clock time; punctuality (both their own and other people's) is particularly important to them. They will want to get their money's worth because they believe that time and value are equivalent. *Through time* people find it easier than *in time* people to plan and make comparisons because they can access different memories simultaneously.

What's important here is knowing which pattern we use. One is no better than the other; they're just different, and both have advantages and disadvantages. It's also important to realize that we can change our preferred timeline, either globally or just for specific occasions. If, for example, you habitually run *in time* patterns, but need to be on time for a series of interviews or meetings, then you can change your patterns to *through time*, just to make sure you get to those important meetings on time.

I'm a *through time* person by nature and I absolutely fit the description above. Being late used to distress me physically. I was once horrendously late for a hospital appointment; my heart and pulse rate were so ridiculously fast that the consultant was convinced that I'd had a serious relapse. The only way I could convince him otherwise was to allow me to go and sit quietly for half-an-hour and then re-test me.

Changing the orientation of your timeline is a relatively simple task. All you need to do is stand up, take a couple of deep breaths, relax and imagine your timeline in its usual place and shape. If you can find a sympathetic soul who's prepared to support your timeline for you while you're working with it, all well and good. If not, you can just as easily do it by yourself.

Visualize your timeline and gently take hold of it. Now move it through an angle of 90° so that, if it used to run through you, it now runs in front of you and vice versa. Remember to be playful and childlike; all we're doing is experimenting with our own experience.

The first time I tried this, I had something of a *Star Trek* experience – and so did Sheila, the lady with whom I was doing the exercise. The dialogue went something like this:

Elaine: *I don't know how to tell you this, but I can't change my timeline because there's a force field in the way.*

Sheila: *I know.*

Elaine: *How do you know?*

Sheila: *Because it's so strong that it's making my arms ache.*

If, like me, you encounter some resistance, then just go inside yourself, identify the part of you that's objecting, and explain that you're just experimenting with a different way of doing things, that you can always revert to your habitual pattern. Carry on doing this until you secure agreement. If necessary, set a time limit for the experiment; agree that at the end of two weeks, say, you'll go back to your original pattern.

Eight years later, Sheila and I still laugh about the experience. It was funny in both senses of the word (haha and peculiar), but it was also fantastic because it helped me to develop the flexibility to change from *through time* to *in time* at will.

This flexibility has enriched my life enormously. *Through time* individuals can be slightly detached from their own experience, and this was certainly true of me. Now, when time isn't an issue and I really want to enjoy whatever it is I'm doing – swimming, cycling, writing, for example – I switch to *in time*. If I'm working to a deadline or getting ready to go out for the evening, I'll default to *through time*.

Knowing that I have a choice over which pattern to use means that I'm now much more relaxed about time than your traditional *through time* person. I still don't like being late but, if circumstances are occasionally against me and I'm not going to be on time, I no longer automatically go into heart attack mode.

Now that you know something about timelines, let's go back to our original task. Just go inside yourself and discover what, if anything, you've left behind at work. If you had a large emotional investment in your job, then it could be a huge chunk of your identity. It may be your sense of self-esteem, self-worth, self-confidence. Only you know. Once you're sure about what it is that you need to retrieve, just put it to one side.

When you're working with timelines, you need to make your timeline a physical reality by laying it down on the floor as a straight line. This may be a poor representation of the way you actually experience your timeline, but this really doesn't matter. By drawing your timeline on the floor and moving along it, you can experience it both kinaesthetically and spatially. You can also step off it and look at it from a different perspective while you gain knowledge, understanding or resources.

Find yourself a room with some space in it – and close the door. Next, think about the span of your life and imagine a line on the floor that represents that span. The day you were born will be at one end; today at the other. I once did some timeline work with an actuary, and he got very – well, actuarial, I suppose – with year zero at one end of the conference room and the day in question at the foot of the whiteboard at the other. There's absolutely no need to be quite that precise. All you need is a straight line that stretches from the past through the present and into the future.

When you know where your line is on the floor and which way it faces (it doesn't matter), stand on it with today behind you. Then walk back to a point on the line that corresponds to you leaving behind at work that part of you that you want to retrieve. Let's imagine it's a sense of belonging, for example. Retrieve it; gather it up; put it back where it belongs – physically, if need be. You're a consenting adult and you're behind a closed door, for goodness' sake.

So, if in our example, your sense of belonging usually sits in the chest, somewhere near to the heart, then you'd pick it up in your hands and physically place them over your chest so that it can return whence it came. Give it a few moments to settle back into its accustomed place. Then notice how you feel.

Now, while you're still on this point on your timeline, check something else. Are you bringing away from work anything that you don't want? The acid test here is usefulness. If your job has given you oodles of self-belief, keep as many of the little blighters in place as you can. If you've got what you came for and you don't need to get rid of anything, then you're done. All you have to do is turn around and walk slowly back up your timeline towards today, noticing what happens as you do so. You're updating your experience now that you've retrieved your sense of belonging.

If, on the other hand, work has given you something that isn't going to serve you well for the remainder of your days – an abiding sense of failure or under-achievement, for example, then here's your opportunity to jettison it. You may be beginning to get the hang of this NLP stuff by now. Go inside yourself and identify what it is that you want to leave behind. Then locate where in your body it is.

It will be there somewhere because our emotions manifest themselves in our bodies. Language reflects this:

That's a load off my shoulders.

That's a weight off my mind.

In much the same way that you can replace something in your body, you can also remove things. You get to choose how that removal takes place. And, depending on the method you choose – and assuming that you have a ready sense of humour – it can actually make you laugh.

If you have a highly developed visual sense, for example, and you've decided that your perceived sense of failure looks like a string of sausages from a Punch and Judy show, you may find yourself pulling them out of your chest, and hurling them into the sea or over a mountain.

I have friends who use water cannon, catapults, geysers. It really doesn't matter what you use, as long as you get rid of the unhelpful whatever it is. And please, please make sure that it's all gone. Imagine that you're having a really thorough spring clean, so look in all the nooks and crannies.

We're almost done, but this last part is really, really important – also really beneficial. Whenever you remove anything, please replace it with something else. Otherwise, there'll be a hole. One of the few things I've retained from school science lessons is that nature abhors a vacuum, so let's not create one.

Again, you're the one in charge so you decide what goes in the space. Make it something positive; something that brings a smile to your face. The laugh of a loved one; the gurgling sounds of your baby; the warmth of the sun on your face; the image of an inspiring person; the feeling of a sense of achievement – you'll know what's right for you. Make the images, sounds and feelings as strong and vivid as you can.

Package all that lovely stuff up in whatever manner seems most appropriate and put it back in its rightful place in your body. Be as playful as you want: stand under a waterfall and let it cascade over you; throw it up in the air above your head like a riot of party-poppers; walk through a scanner at the airport and feel the beams. All you have to do at the end is know that it's now replaced the unhelpful sense that was there before.

To finish, turn around and walk slowly back up your timeline towards today, noticing what happens as you do so. You're updating your experience now that you're different. You're also in a much fitter state to embark on the next phase of your life – whatever it is.

Chapter X

Having a spring clean

PDJ

Every behaviour has a positive intention.

Spring cleaning's not what it once was. It's probably down to the advent of central heating, vacuum cleaners, floor-to-floor carpeting and dual-income households.

I remember going to my grandmother's house in the 1960s when spring cleaning was what it once was: a huge annual event. It involved moving all the furniture, rolling up all the rugs and beating them over the clothes line (my preferred task), taking down the curtains, opening all the windows, scrubbing, mopping, dusting, using proprietary cleaning products that would fall foul of health and safety today, polishing with newspaper, vinegar and lemon and, of course, drinking copious quantities of tea from an industrial-sized teapot.

By the end of the day, the house looked, smelt and felt fresh, new and ready for the year ahead. And that was absolutely the point of it. And that's the point of what we're doing next. Now that we've cleared out all that negative redundancy gunk, we may as well continue with our internal spring cleaning.

By the time we've reached adulthood, it's more than likely that we've been through any number of experiences that we've filed away in our memories under the negative tab. Whenever we react in a way that we don't really understand in the here and now, you can bet your bottom dollar it's because we've reconnected with the memory of one of these events. The official term for these is trigger events.

What I love about working with trigger events is that clients have absolutely no idea that that's what they are. Sometimes, they can barely even consciously remember the event in question. Here's an example.

Tom, a client with a slight stammer, shipped up. He was doing really well in corporate life, but the further he advanced up the ladder, the more public speaking he had to do. The more public speaking he had to do, the more he stammered. Tom had tried everything from a voice coach to sheer force of will, but nothing had worked. He came to me in desperation.

In an inspired moment, I asked him if he'd always stammered. He'd clearly never considered this before.

I'm not sure but I have a feeling that, as a young child, I didn't.

A swift mobile phone call to his older sister confirmed this. I asked him to lay down a timeline, reconnect with the feeling he had when he stammered, and then walk down the timeline to the point at which he acquired the stammer.

Elaine: *How old are you?*

Tom: *Eight or so.*

Elaine: *Where are you?*

Tom: *On a school camping trip.*

Elaine: *What's happening?*

Tom: *I've woken up in the middle of the night and one of the adult helpers is standing by the side of my bed.*

Tom hadn't thought about this incident in years, but he vividly remembered getting home and wanting to tell his parents about it. He never did though: he was so nervous that he simply couldn't get the words out of his mouth.

In his memory, Tom had created an automatic association between the camping trip, nerves and not being able to articulate properly. Years later, whenever he became nervous – as he did before speaking in public, the memory triggered the automatic response.

Once we'd identified the camping trip as the trigger event, all we had to do was change the machine code of that particular memory. We did that by using a technique called change personal history (see below). We replaced the negative anchor of the trip with a positive one made up of resources that would have helped the eight-year old Tom to deal with the incident.

The three resources Tom chose were the loving relationship he had with his girlfriend, the sense of being safe, and confidence in himself and his abilities. We created a circle of excellence comprising these three resources (see chapter VII). Next, Tom walked back up his timeline, updating his experience. Finally, he indulged in a spot of future pacing which, as you no doubt remember from chapter VII, is just another term for a cocktail of mental rehearsal and maximum vividness.

In Tom's case, I asked him to imagine the next occasion when he knew he would be speaking in public, to associate fully into that occasion, to see, hear and feel everything as intensely as possible, and just notice what was going on for him.

As always with NLP, the proof of the technique is in the behaving. Last time I heard from him, Tom was still flying up the corporate ladder, taking public speaking in his stride.

In the case of inexplicable (to us) reactions, it's important to realize that the behaviour is only a symptom, not the issue itself. In the example above, Tom's stammering – troublesome as he found it – was no more than a manifestation of his memory's filing system.

I don't know either what your trigger events are or what behavioural incapacity they've given you, but your subconscious does. Mine certainly did. I used to have a crippling fear of rejection; so crippling that it made me incapable of ever taking the initiative with other people. Had I asked someone to do something with me, and they'd refused, my sense of rejection would have been unbearable. So I didn't ask.

In an NLP training session, I traced this back to an incident that seemed trivial on the surface but had a massive emotional charge underneath. I was six and was participating in some grand family reunion. All the uncles, aunts, cousins, grandparents were there, and we were walking to a restaurant. Overcome by the noise and the numbers, I wanted the reassurance of holding my mother's hand. Her hands were full of my newly arrived baby brother, and she directed me towards an ample-bosomed aunt.

It's so insignificant a moment that you can't even really classify it as an event. Looking at it through adult eyes, I understand that my mother was undoubtedly tired and preoccupied with the baby, and probably took the view that, as a relatively mature six-year-old, I was more than capable of just taking things in my stride.

I got through the reunion without making a fuss, but made a connection in my memory between reaching out to another person and rejection that directed my behaviour for decades. Now that I've changed the machine code of that memory in the same way as I did with Tom, it's become completely ho-hum without any emotional charge whatsoever. More liberatingly, I often invite people to do all sorts of things with me; some of them even agree. And even if they don't, that's absolutely fine with me.

If you'd like to free yourself from the shackles of a trigger event, here's how I do change personal history:

1 Lay down your timeline.

2 Reconnect with the negative feeling and walk down your timeline until you know you're at the point at which you experienced this feeling for the very first time.

3 Step off your timeline so that you gain a new perspective on the trigger event. Ask yourself: What resources did I need then?

4 When you've found three resources, create yourself a circle of excellence (see chapter VII).

5 Step back onto your timeline and fire the positive anchor you created in your circle.

6 Walk slowly back up your timeline, updating your experience as you go and noticing what's different.

7 Step off your timeline and bring the trigger event to mind. If it's completely ho-hum, you're done: go directly to step 8. If it still feels negative, find some more resources and repeat steps 4 to 7, before proceeding to step 8.

8 Future pace (see chapter VII).

The version of change personal history that I learned involved pressing people's knees which was never going to fit comfortably with coaching in corporate life. I ended up only using the technique with those corporate clients whom I instinctively felt wouldn't class it as sexual harassment.

Then came the day when I needed to use it with a male client who had very chubby knees. Looking at those knees, I just knew that I wasn't going to be able to do it. Nothing to do with the client; all about my attitude towards obesity which I'm glad to say that I've now tackled.

In the moment, I realized that I would have to find another way of working, and I did. I brought timelines into the equation. This taught me a very useful lesson: there isn't a right or a wrong way of doing things with NLP, and you really can mix and match to your heart's content. Imagine yourself back at that sweetie counter in your local Woolworths'.

There isn't a manual that we have to follow religiously. In this respect, NLP is similar to daily living: we just do the best we can, making use of whatever comes to hand in our mental and behavioural toolbox. That toolbox is now larger than it was, so let's remember to use it. Everything we've learned thus far will help us to have more choice, more flexibility, more control over ourselves and how we interact with the world. That's a pretty good jumping off point for part II of this book.

Part II

Getting On With The Rest Of Our Life

Chapter XI

Being who we are

PDJ

We are not our behaviour.

As I explained way back in chapter I, our identity and our behaviour are two completely different things, even though we sometimes choose to make them equivalent. We often tell others what we do when they ask us who we are. So who are we now that we've temporarily stopped doing what we used to do?

It's an absolutely fundamental question, and how we answer it will determine how we approach the task of finding our new niche in life. My electrician Shaun recently told me two very different tales of redundancy among his customers.

The first concerned a caretaker in his 60s who realized that, at his age and with his lack of professional qualifications, he wasn't going to get another job. So he didn't waste time looking. Instead, he asked himself one simple question:

What else can I do?

It turned out that he's always been a dab hand with a paint pot and brush. So he started by asking his neighbours if they needed any painting and decorating doing. They did. News of his prowess and prices spread through the neighbourhood. Hey presto, he's fully employed again. OK, he's not going to be the next Richard Branson, but he's happier than he ever was in his caretaking days.

The second victim of the angel with the axe was a high-flying corporate banker. Big house, bonuses, Beamer, beautiful young wife: this guy appeared to have everything – except the ability to deal with redundancy. His response was to put an end to it all. He'd conflated who he was with what he did so completely that, without his job, his life had no meaning,

Admittedly, this is an extreme example. However, it may not be that easy to answer the question about who we are now, particularly if we've come to the end of a long stint in corporate life. Since I unceremoniously left corporate life two years ago, I've realized that I was never cut out for it: altogether too eccentric to ever fit comfortably. Yes, well, I've said elsewhere in this book that I can be a tad slow.

Since I've been out, I've had a growing sensation of liberating myself from one of those whale-boned instruments of torture: a Victorian corset. Every so often, I take a deep breath, and the lacings loosen and the panels release. I'm growing more into myself because I no longer have to conform to someone else's idea of what a senior manager is, does, looks like, behaves, feels or says. I can just be me.

Don't get me wrong. I'm not dissing corporate life here; I'm just pointing out that it may not be for all of us. It may be that what it gives us is worth what it takes from us, but I don't think we should be under any illusions about the price that we're paying for the privilege of belonging. There can often be a huge disconnect between who we are – or could be – and the version of us that shows up in corporate life. Think about your CV for a couple of moments. How good a representation is that document of the real you?

It's absolutely none of my business what you choose to do next, and if you opt to head straight back to corporatedo(o)m, all well and good. All I'm doing in this chapter is highlighting a few ways in which you can gain some different perspectives on who you really are.

Let's start with a provocative thought. Friend Jason gave me a book when he came to lunch the other day. A few days later, I read:

One form of resistance is to be close to what you'd love to do, but not quite doing it. You are in the vicinity of it, but standing in the shadows. My own example was when I was involved in running one of the world's premier mind body spirit lecture series in London...Then it dawned on me, "I don't want to be the one organizing the talks anymore, I want to be the one giving the talks!"[21]

Not quite what I had in mind when I wanted to work with racing cars...

The reason I identified so strongly with that is that I've spent my career writing things for and as other people, giving elegant expression to their voices, but never to my own. Was I pursuing a shadow career? You bet. Are you? Only you know. Me, I'm not doing that any more. Now that I'm out of corporate life, I've found my own voice and I'm relishing writing as myself. My blogs and three short stories are already out there, and more books are bursting to get out of my head just as soon as I'm done here.

Back to the task of unearthing who we really are. One of my all-time favourite ways of discovering more about ourselves is an exercise that I did when I was doing my coaching training with ITS.[22] Assuming that you're not a hermit and that you have at least five proper friends, it's remarkably easy. All you have to do is identify between five and eight people who know you really well and ask them to jot down what they see as your unique abilities, your special qualities.

To make the results as rich and revealing as possible, pick people from different areas of your life: family, old friend, new friend, colleague, gym buddy, fellow club member. If my results were fairly typical – which, of course, they may not have been – then you'll read some things about yourself that you've always known and some that come as a complete surprise.

For example:

You clearly have a strong set of values and principles.

You have a great sense of humour with a keen eye for life's absurdities.

You are a great networker both at work and in the rest of your life and are good at making things happen by utilizing your contacts and people you know.

You have a light and fun way of connecting, but still keep things meaningful.

The first two of those I already knew; the second two were news to me.

Moving along, if you've recently come out of corporate life, you've probably been Myers-Briggsed to death. You probably know your four-letter combination (INFP; ESTJ; and so on) as well as career soldiers know their army number. Nothing wrong with Myers-Briggs; it can give us some really useful insights into our behavioural preferences. Being the eccentric soul that I am though, I was never particularly happy at being lumped into one of 16 groups with a load of other people.

Fortunately, just recently, I've come across some other resources that give us even more valuable insights. One of these resources is Grant Henderson who, together with his parents, has developed a wonderfully insightful system called i3 profiling.[23]

The three i's in question are our individual instinctive indicators. Unlike most other profiling or personality assessment tools, i3 doesn't put us into predetermined personality types or quadrants because it recognizes that we're all different. Not only do you get a profile that's unique to you, the other bonus is that a qualified profiler goes through your profile with you over the phone.

If you want to have some kind of idea of the extent of the difference between Myers-Briggs and i3, the former told me that I'm a nurturer; the latter told me that:

You're a highly motivational leader whose common sense, entrepreneurial approach and advice is of great value to the people around you.

I'm only recommending this to you because I found it enormously helpful and because I have a huge personal and professional regard for what Grant's doing.

Alternatively or additionally, if you go to www.authentichappiness.org, you can take any number of surveys. The one I'm commending to you here is the *Values in Action Survey of Character Strengths.*[24] It takes approximately 25 minutes to complete, and ranks 24 of your strengths ranging from humour, industry, and leadership through to social intelligence, self-control, and creativity.

In the book[25] that amplifies the survey results, Martin Seligman suggests that we use our top five signature strengths:

every day in the main realms of (y)our life to bring abundant gratification and authentic happiness.

One of the things I love about NLP is that it encourages us to look to both the external and the internal world and to pay attention to the information that we're receiving from both sources. So, now that you've collected and considered feedback from the external world, I'd like you to turn your attention inwards. This is a source of information that we often ignore.

Coming up is an exercise that can reveal to you things about yourself that you may not know. You can try doing it by yourself, but it may work best first time around if you find a friend to help you. It's not an onerous task; all the friend has to do is ask you two questions repeatedly in a curious, non-judgemental tone. This is absolutely not the time to have an investigative journalist or crime-busting police professional on your side.

I realize that, as adults, some of us find it difficult to follow simple instructions, but this is one of those occasions where doing so is the best policy. Adopt whatever role model will help you to do exactly as you're told. The two questions are:

What do you want?

and

What will that do for you?

The two of you keep going round the loop, allowing as much time as is necessary for each answer to inform the next. This is effectively an exploration into the intentions behind your behaviour. Eventually, you'll reach an intention that is so fundamental and meaningful to you that you'll know when you're done.

You'll also be aware – perhaps for the first time – of the highest intention of your behaviour. This will chime with your values and will be really important to you in your map of the world. This is an invaluable piece of information for you as you seek to be yourself in the next phase of your life.

To make it easier to understand, here's a real life example from my corporate coaching days. I was working with Tony who was feeling extremely disgruntled with corporate life because he'd been passed over for promotion – again. He didn't know what he wanted to do. He was in that Clash frame of mind:

Should I stay or should I go?

Elaine: *So what do you want?*

Tony: *A job where I feel fulfilled.*

Elaine: *What will feeling fulfilled do for you?*

Tony: *Make me feel as though I'm contributing in some way.*

Elaine: *So what do you want?*

Tony: *I've just told you. I want to know that I've made a difference.*

Elaine: *What will knowing that you've made a difference do for you?*

Tony: *Honour my need to serve others.*

Elaine: *So what do you want?*

Tony: *I want to honour that need, either within this job or somewhere else.*

Elaine: *And what will honouring that need do for you?*

Tony: *Let me know that I'm being true to myself, that I'm being more of myself.*

Tony's last response was about as highly valued a criterion as you can get, yet it was a revelation to him that, at his core, he had this deep-seated need and desire to serve others. He was in his early 40s, he'd spent his entire career to date in business, and hadn't been involved in any type of voluntary or charitable work since his student days.

What had started out as an internal debate about his career path turned into an exploration of how he could be true to himself. Fortunately, the organization for which we worked had a very active community engagement programme. Within a couple of months, Tony was both mentoring pupils at a local school and helping with an adult literacy programme some weekends. Once he realized that his frustration with work had more to do with his lack of personal fulfilment than with work in its own right, his career also flourished. Tony earned promotion a year later.

Before we come to the end of this chapter, let's move over to the dark side (only kidding). There's more about working with your unconscious in the next chapter. For now, please reacquaint yourself with your timeline (flip back to chapter IX if you need a refresher) because I want you to take a little trip in both directions.

First, walk down your timeline to your childhood self. As you re-connect with your younger self, re-connect with the dreams, ambitions and passions that you had then. Are they evident in your present, or are they present only as a largely unacknowledged emotional tug of what might have been? If they're still important to you, set your unconscious mind the task of considering what role they could play in your current circumstances.

Next, walk up your timeline until you're ten, 15, 20 years in the future, look back at your life during that time and ask yourself:

How do I wish I'd been in that intervening period? How would I like to have shown up in my own life?

Again, ask your unconscious mind to consider the possibilities of how you could bring those desires into play in your life. You don't need to cudgel your brains and give yourself a headache here. It's not a question of trying; if anything, it's the exact opposite. It's a question of being aware of the responses when they arrive and being open enough to accept and consider them – whatever they are.

This is just more information about ourselves that we can chuck into the pot as we work out exactly what it is that we want to do with the rest of our life.

Chapter XII

Learning to inkle

> ## PDJ
>
> *Our unconscious mind is benevolent.*

During the writing of this book, no animals were harmed. No sorry, that's not what I meant. I'll start again. During the writing of this book, I had the good fortune to watch a fascinating *Horizon* programme on UK television channel, BBC2.[26] Its subject was the unconscious; its range was astonishing. It had everything from knitters in brain scanners and golfers with faulty putting technique to radio-tagged ants as neurons.

Brain experts in Arizona, Columbia, London, Montreal and Oxford have all, by a myriad of different routes, come to the same conclusion. Far from being the lowly, primal seat of suppressed desires and even darker instincts, the unconscious is in fact a sophisticated powerhouse that designs and implements rapid and efficient strategies.

Wow, we've got a sophisticated powerhouse on our side before we even start. Sounds good to me; let's crack on. Thanks to part I of this book, we've already developed the habit of working with our unconscious. All we'll be doing here is refining those skills still further, learning to pay even greater attention to our innermost inklings.

I've been aware of inklings for some time. What I didn't know until today is that inkle exists as a verb. Thefreedictionary.com defines it as:

to communicate in an undertone or whisper, to give a hint of something, hence inkling.

I'd only previously heard it on the BBC television programme *Eggheads* where Daphne Fowler uses it as a noun in the sense of a tiny inkling.

To say that I know where I stand on the question of inklings would be an absolutely massive understatement: I'm as pro as it's possible to be. I speak as the person who has just applied to Royal Mail to have my house christened *Inklings.* When my leaded lights window project gets under way, the word will be appearing in all its glory in the transom window above my front door.

You're probably wondering why I'm such a huge fan. The answer's simple: inklings are not only the promptings of our unconscious mind, they're also an incredibly valuable source of information. Until we learn just how valuable they are, I think we have a tendency to ignore them. It may be that Monsieur Descartes' influence is still flowing down the centuries, imprinting us with a belief that leads us to devalue and dismiss anything that isn't a conscious, logical thought.

There may be something else at work here too. These days, it's all too easy to spend vast swathes of time engaged with electronic gadgetry – iPhone, iPad, iPod, Kindle, MP3 player. Nothing wrong with that in moderation, but being permanently plugged in can draw us away not only from the external world, but also from our internal experience.

As a strategy, distraction has its place. If you're in pain, and you want to be less aware of the degree of hurt, then distracting yourself by whatever method works for you is an excellent idea. However, if you frequently feel the need to distract yourself, then you may be distracting yourself from your own life, which tends to raise some uncomfortable issues about how you're spending your allotted span on the planet. Learning how to inkle with yourself could be a great place to start.

Even if we're in the habit of ignoring our inklings, we all know how they manifest themselves – in either pictures, words or feelings. I rather suspect that they conform to our leading rep system. I think we also know how we dismiss them. I used to bat most of mine away without a second's thought; the only exception I made was when I met people for the first time. In this situation, I used to trust my inklings absolutely.

What I'm talking about here is using your sensory acuity on yourself. If your inklings are screaming at you to stay away from someone or something, there'll be a very good reason for it. For instance, the only time I ever reversed a decision that my inklings had made for me about a person led to unease, unpleasantness, and heartache – not just for me, but for a number of my colleagues as well.

Although I acknowledge that the other person was doing the best she could, I also know, with the benefit of hindsight, that my inklings went into overdrive when we first met because our values and ways of being in the world were so fundamentally different that a happy ending was never on the cards. This was one of those lessons that will be with me for the remainder of my days. Now I honour my inklings with the respect they deserve.

If you're an habitual non-inkler, then you may have to pay close attention to yourself to catch your inklings as and when they occur. First step is to know what form they take, so you know exactly what it is you're trying to catch. Be aware too that your conscious mind generally steps in immediately, only too eager to despatch your inklings into oblivion as rapidly as possible.

I've been heeding my innermost promptings for eight years now, and this to-and-fro between my conscious and unconscious mind continues to this day. Here's a recent example relating to health. I have a history of headaches which admittedly have been much better since I saw an eccentric to the point of nutty professor two years ago. They'd been troublesome lately though, so I discussed them with coach Teak:

Teak: *What message are the headaches giving you?*

Elaine: *I don't know.*

I mentally added a *yet* to my response, in the hope that something would dawn on me later. It did. I was standing in my bedroom, looking down at my bed when something I hadn't thought of in years came into my mind.

One of the first coaching books I ever read tells the story of a man with stomach pains for which there was no medical explanation.[27] His condition stumped the doctors for the simple reason that it wasn't a medical problem. He'd got into the habit of wearing his trousers belt too tightly. I think the story only stuck in my memory because it struck me as slightly silly.

My conscious mind was about to dismiss it again, when an insistent little inkle demanded that I pay attention. I continued looking down at the bed; my eyes alighted on the single, flat pillow.

I've had a visceral dislike of big pillows, fat pillows, double pillows ever since early childhood. Until very recently, I took a childish delight in throwing them overboard whenever I found them on guest beds. It used to drive my mother wild; in her map of the world, beds always had two plump pillows.

Could my pillow be contributing towards my headaches?

No sooner was the inkling grasped than my conscious mind jumped right in – vociferously:

Don't be so bloody ridiculous! As if it could be that simple!

Surely it's worth an experiment for a night or two, pleaded my intimidated inkling.

My headaches are now much less frequent and much less intense, and are usually explicable by external factors such as a cold or over-indulgence. These stories are prime examples of just how much valuable information is out of conscious awareness yet available to us via our inklings.

Back to the big picture stuff. Now that we're ready to start thinking about our new niche in life, the big question is:

What could we possibly do next?

I think there's a huge hint in that *possibly*. Remember the recycling ads on the tele with the tagline of *the possibilities are endless?* That's what we're going for here, and we absolutely don't want or need any interference from the logical, left hand-side of the brain – thank you very much.

One of the best ways of communicating with our inklings is to go into a light trance. I sometimes work as a hypnotherapist[28], so I'm very aware that some of us can be very prejudicial towards trances. In my map of the world, this is a mere misunderstanding. We all go into and out of trance every day of our lives.

Anyone who's worked in corporate life will have been in a trance at some stage during a business presentation – unless the speaker was exceptionally talented and went out of his or her way to use particularly colourful language that engaged our senses.

On a more positive note, when we're busy doing what we love doing – reading, painting, writing, model-making, flower arranging – we become so engrossed in what we're doing that the external world ceases to exist for us. This too is a trance.

With my writer's hat firmly on my head, I can hardly fail to have noticed that our language demonstrates our absence from the real world and our entry into trance:

I was miles away.

Sorry, I'd tuned out of what's been going on.

I was away with the fairies.

Contrary to popular belief, there's absolutely nothing wrong with keeping company with fairies. It used to bother me slightly that I could cycle huge chunks of my journey home from the office without any conscious memory of having done so. I realize now that while part of my mind was paying attention to the traffic conditions and keeping me safe, another part had gone deeply into trance. Often, by the time I arrived home, I'd have the answer to some creative conundrum that I'd been struggling with all day.

Trances are both perfectly normal and purposeful. They can be very helpful as the gateway to discovering things about ourselves that we either don't know, half-know or don't want to know. No need to panic: it's only information about ourselves, internal feedback if you like, and we're under absolutely no obligation to act on the information. We may want to though if it's going to help move us from where we are currently to where we want to be.

There are any number of ways in which you can engage more with your inner experience, enter trance-like states more often, and be more aware of your inklings. It's an intensely personal experiment, so I genuinely don't know what will work for you. Here are some ideas.

Lose yourself in some form of physical exercise. In my experience, swimming, yoga, dancing, cycling and walking (without being plugged into anything) all facilitate communing with your inner self. American poet and philosopher Henry David Thoreau said of walking:

I am not where my body is – I am out of my senses.

Yes, that's exactly the sensation we want: go for it.

Start paying attention to stories wherever you find them – legends, myths, fairy tales, children's books, radio and television drama, films – and particularly to the metaphors they use. Aristotle knew a thing or two and one of them is that:

metaphor is halfway between the unintelligible and the commonplace.

When I was doing my NLP training with ITS[29], one of the most entertaining and illuminating exercises we did was to get into groups of three and rotate the following three roles between us:

Person 1*:* [start the round by saying] *Life is like…*

Person 2: [complete the metaphor]*…a bowl of cherries…a horror film*

Person 3: [supply the rationale]*…because it looks good, tastes good, and does you good…because you don't know what's coming next, but you do know it's going to be nasty.*

If two people were actually using those metaphors in relation to life, their daily experiences would be radically different.

You can also engage more with non-verbal modes of expression. I regularly go and look at all forms of art – paintings, sculpture, video installations – because I find it deeply meditative and stimulating. We have the great good fortune to live in a country where we can go and do this for free.

More daringly, give it a go yourself, and ignore absolutely, completely and utterly your conscious mind telling you that you can't do whatever it is. This has nothing whatsoever to do with being good at art or producing a masterpiece; it's all about becoming more familiar with more of yourself.

At coach Teak's suggestion, during the writing of this book, I allocated 30 minutes a day to drawing – an activity to which I had a deep-seated aversion thanks to the art teacher at school. At that point, I was in the darkest depths of part I: something wasn't quite right, but I didn't know what that *something* was.

In ways I don't even begin to understand, that one small act of drawing – or doodling or scribbling, which would be more accurate terms – stimulated both my creativity and the communication between my conscious and unconscious mind. I had a whole gaggle of inklings telling me to take time off from the book (yes, I've just decided that the collective noun for inklings is gaggle; at rest, obviously; if they were in flight, they'd be a skein – as with geese).

It wasn't easy; the Protestant work ethic is too firmly embedded in my psyche for that. I felt as though I was playing hooky, especially when my inklings insisted I take a break for a whole three days.

When I took up my pen again, it was as though my brain had spent the intervening days in a battery charger. Not only did the words flow, they flowed in different streams simultaneously.

Oh, I don't have to finish chapter 6 before I move onto chapter 7? I can be in the middle of three chapters at once?

I also saw what had been bugging me: a whole chapter was missing. I wrote it at one sitting. Through doodling, I've learnt an invaluable lesson: writing doesn't have to linear. I'm now in the middle of parts II, III and IV of this book, and am flitting happily between them. It's a perfect demonstration of the PDJ for chapter VIII:

having choice is better than not having choice.

I think the whole point of these various activities is that we're mindful whilst we're doing them. I looked up mindfulness on the internet and came across this:

Mindfulness means paying attention in a particular way; on purpose, in the present moment, and non-judgmentally.[30]

Those are the words of Jon Kabat-Zinn, teacher of mindfulness meditation and the founder of the Mindfulness-Based Stress Reduction programme at the University of Massachusetts Medical Center.

Perhaps mindfulness works because it's about being rather than doing. Let's not overlook the fact that we're human beings, not human doings. When you're a tad more familiar with trances and inklings and have more access to your inner self than was previously the case, ask yourself:

what would I do if all things were possible for me and I knew that I couldn't fail?

Let your imagination, inklings and the right side of your brain run riot and see what surfaces. Whatever it is, keep hold of it. Regard it as a priceless piece of information as we turn our thoughts to what it is we want to do next in life.

Chapter XIII

Working out what we really, really want

PDJ

Human behaviour is purposeful.

Whatever your view of the Spice Girls, we're going to be doing serious work around some of the *Wannabe* lyrics in this chapter. By the end of it, I want you to be able to:

tell me what you want, what you really, really want.

While we're in the lyrics, can we just do a reality check to make sure that you've left your past well and truly behind you, and you're firmly focused on the future? To misquote, but only to the extent of personal pronouns:

If you want your future, forget your past.

If something about your past is still bothering you, please return to part I and do whatever you need to get yourself in the right state.

Now I don't know about you, but for me there used to be something *not quite nice* (as one set of über-posh neighbours would have had it) about asking for things. This included the mere act of asking myself what I really wanted in life. Well, I've got an update on this one. It turns out that there's a lot of truth in the old adage that:

If you don't ask, you don't get.

This chapter is all about working out exactly what it is that we want from this next phase of our life. It's all about outcome orientation which, if you can remember that far back, is one of the four pillars of NLP that I referred to right at the beginning of the book.

As we come to terms with redundancy, we'll have any number of long- and short-term goals: securing an income, keeping our family together, meeting our financial obligations, finding something more satisfying to do, and so on.

Praiseworthy as these are, they are absolutely not the same as outcomes. Goals are something to which you aspire; outcomes are something that you create. The main difference between them is that outcomes are so much more specific. You know when you've created an outcome because you can see it, hear it, and feel it.

Depending on what it is, you can sometimes even taste it and smell it, as was the case with a friend of mine whose outcome was to cook the perfect risotto. The level of perfection she was striving for eluded the rest of us, but we were happy to eat our way through the various levels of non-perfection.

She knew, down to the minutest level of detail, exactly what she wanted. This is a pivotal piece of learning: if you don't know what you want, you have absolutely no chance of getting it. It is, of course, one of the harshest lessons of childhood that we don't always get what we want anyway; sometimes unforeseen circumstances intervene and sometimes we let ourselves down. The fact still remains: if you do know what you want, you significantly increase your chances of getting it.

Now I realize that, for most of us, thinking about what we want is usually confined to those few alcohol-enhanced moments before the clock strikes midnight on New Year's Eve. That's when we make resolutions for the year ahead and, as a general rule, we're so inept at keeping them that they return for a repeat performance the next year, and the year after, and the year after that. I used to have a work colleague who vowed to give up smoking when his daughter was born; she's now in her first year at university. My ex-colleague still smokes; so does his daughter.

One of the reasons for our inability to keep resolutions may well be that we're culturally attuned to noticing what isn't working and then apportioning blame rather than to noticing what is working and then apportioning praise. There's a world of difference between asking yourself:

What's the problem?

and

What outcome do I want?

The first question keeps you firmly stuck in the present, in the here and now of the situation; the second one takes you into the future, to a place where you can reflect calmly on what you want.

Confrontations are a rare occurrence in my life these days, but I did – unwittingly and with the best of intentions – find myself in the middle of one last summer. It had the potential to be extremely upsetting because it involved someone with whom I've had a professional relationship for eight years and whom I now count as a friend. It all started with a misunderstanding as to whether I'd cancelled an appointment or not.

In a spirit of helpfulness, I sent an email with what I intended to be constructive feedback. Unfortunately, in the eyes of the recipient, it was an unwarranted complaint, and elicited what I regarded as a totally over-the-top response. I found myself reading a legalistic letter, the tone of which completely ignored our long-standing relationship.

As my fingers hovered over the keyboard, I managed to suppress the response rage that was threatening to engulf me and ask myself that crucial question:

What outcome do I want?

I knew that I wanted to have a continuing – and mutually beneficial – relationship with a fellow professional, so I refrained from telling him where to stick his professional services. Instead, I responded in a light-hearted yet respectful manner, making it obvious that I intended to turn up for my next appointment, in spite of the spat.

That first encounter wasn't particularly easy; we both had to make an effort to normalize relations. Thanks to outcome orientation though, we've been able to build on that fragile peace and get ourselves back to where we were.

Outcome thinking has three basic elements:

- know your present situation: where you are now;

- know your desired situation: where you want to be; and

- plan your strategy: how to get from one to the other, using either the resources you have or creating new ones.

If we apply this model to my professional spat, my present situation was being on the brink of ending the relationship, my desired situation was to maintain that relationship, and my strategy entailed using my resources of rapport-building, respect and humour to get from one to the other.

In NLP, truly effective outcomes have six little friends for company. These are known as the well-formedness conditions. I know the phrase doesn't exactly roll off the tongue, even when you're reading to yourself, but bear with me. This is really useful stuff. Let's meander through the six conditions one-by-one.

Stated in the positive

This is especially interesting because some of us have an ingrained habit of talking about what we want in the negative:

I want to lose weight.

I want to give up smoking.

This is a habit with failure woven into its DNA because in order not to do something such as over-eating or having another cigarette, we have to think about doing it, so we know what not to do. Try telling yourself not to think about a brown cow. See what I mean?

The last thought I had before my near-fatal cycling accident was:

Don't go anywhere near that nasty drainage ditch.

I should have known that in order to process that thought, my brain would first need to think about going there. Although I have no memory of the incident whatsoever, my body clearly followed my brain.

If you have an outcome that's framed negatively, turn it into a positive by asking yourself:

What do I want instead?

In the examples above, it could be:

I want to look great in skinny jeans.

I want to be healthier and have more money at the end of each month.

Demonstrable in sensory experience

This one links back to the rep systems we got to know in part I. Ask yourself:

How will I know when I've achieved my outcome?

What will I be seeing, hearing and feeling?

What will my partner or best friend be seeing me doing and hearing me saying?

This is the evidence procedure for your outcome. Think of young children in the back of a car:

Are we there yet?

Capable of being achieved with the available resources

Remember the vast array of things that you can use as resources? If not, flip back to chapter VII and refresh your memory. Just take some time and consider what resources you'll need to achieve your outcome.

Some outcomes relate only to you. This is particularly the case if you're working on some aspect of your own development. If your outcome is to become more outgoing, for instance, that doesn't really involve anyone else. However, you may want to pick a role model and use that person as one of your resources, and you'll certainly want to pay attention to the feedback that your new outgoing personality is eliciting from the people around you.

Although we can try and have as much of our outcome under our own control as possible, most of us are in a system of one sort or another (see chapter II). So it's eminently possible that we'll need to involve the other people in our system. If this is the case, then you need to consider your outcome from their point of view. You know how to do this now. Just go to second position. Ask yourself:

What do I need to do to encourage others to help me achieve my outcome?

What's in it for them?

Be mindful too of the fact that achieving our outcome will undoubtedly have a ripple effect on the other people in our system, so do discuss it with them in advance. Also, make sure that it relates to the larger outcomes that are important both to you and to the other members of your system.

Capable of being achieved in an appropriate context

This one entails the use of both common sense and imagination because you need to make your outcome as specific as you possibly can. Let's start with the common sense approach. It's probably best to ask yourself at least four basic questions:

When do I want this outcome?

Where do I want this outcome?

With whom do I want this outcome?

For how long do I want this outcome?

Money's a good example. You may well want to limit your spending as much as you reasonably can during this temporary transition. That's a perfectly appropriate outcome, given the circumstances; continuing with it once your income's flowing again would be inappropriate. That would only keep you in a place of frugality when you could be in one of abundance.

Let's move right along to the imaginative part of the exercise. Engage your imagination to see, hear and feel (as appropriate) your outcome in as much detail as you can.

A couple of years ago, I had to move. I wasted a lot of time looking at relatively modern houses and flats that were never going to ring my bell, but I didn't know that at the time. The moment I brought my imagination into the equation and started visualizing what I wanted, I knew exactly what it was: a pre-war house with a garden. Did I study history at university? Yes. Do I love old things? Yes. Do I love being outside in my own space? Yes. Was my all-time favourite house the 1930s mid-terrace I lived in until I was six? Yes. Doh!

The more specific you make your outcome, the more real it will become.

Capable of retaining positive by-products

The mere fact that you've created an outcome that you want to achieve means that you're about to change your present situation in one way or another. That puts your current positive by-products at risk. These are another of those entities that lurk just below the surface, that we're not really aware of until we think about them consciously.

To demonstrate the power of positive by-products, I shall revert to the much maligned social pariahs of our day: smokers. On my first NLP training course, we managed to list 42 positive by-products of smoking. The well-known ones were much in evidence:

It helps me relax.

It enables me to think my way through problems.

It puts me at my ease in social situations.

It gives my hands something to do.

But so too were much more esoteric and unexpected ones.

It gives me a break from my girlfriend's nagging because I'm not allowed to smoke in the house.

Standing at the garden gate and having a cigarette is the only bit of me time that I get each day.

Perhaps the most poignant example of a positive by-product of smoking is a tale that NLP training supremo Ian McDermott of ITS[31] relates. During a coffee break at a conference, a woman came and sat down next to him and asked if she could smoke. He nodded.

Ian: *Have you smoked since childhood?*

Woman: *No, I took it up in my 40s.*

Ian: *How come?*

Woman: *I had a very dear friend who was the person I was closest to on the planet, even closer than I am to my husband. She was an inveterate smoker and died of cancer.*

Ian: *Isn't that a reason for not taking it up?*

Woman: *Logically yes, but for me smoking is a way of bringing her back. When I strike the match, light the cigarette, inhale and smell the smoke, it's as though she's beside me again.*

See what I mean about the potential power? This was a positive by-product that completely and utterly defies logic. The woman had experienced profound loss caused by smoking. She was under absolutely no illusions as to the potential health risks she was running by taking it up. But the emotional pull of feeling that she was with her friend again was irresistible.

This, by the way, is why so many well-intended attempts to change bad habits fail. Unless we find some other means of satisfying the positive intentions of the positive by-products associated with our former behaviour, we'll find it very difficult to change that behaviour permanently.

Once you're identified what positive by-products are at risk for you, get creative. Work out how you can incorporate them into your outcome so that you keep what's good and purposeful about your current situation.

Ecologically sound

This one relates to keeping your system in balance. It's an internal check you perform to make sure that your outcome is worth the time, money and effort that it's going to cost you, and is also in keeping with your sense of self. We often overlook this last item. If my experience is anything to go by, that's a daft thing to do.

Much earlier in life, I allowed an employment agency to put my name forward for a job with a tobacco company, in spite of my aversion to smoking. I jumped through all the hoops: completed the tests, went through the interviews – and got the job. Everyone was pleased as Punch for me, but I simply couldn't bring myself to sign the paperwork and accept the job.

With the benefit of hindsight and NLP, I know that happened because my core value is respect. In my case, this includes respecting how I treat my body. I'm not passing any judgements here; all I'm highlighting is the fact that we all have values that drive our behaviour. You may not even know what yours are; I certainly didn't.

What you will know though is when you're contravening them. You'll feel a huge sense of incongruence, of your system telling you, in words, pictures or feelings, depending on your lead rep system:

this isn't right somehow.

Congruence is that feeling of wholeness, of being in absolute harmony with ourselves; incongruence is the exact opposite. We all have internal signals that are completely involuntary that tell us whether we're congruent or not. Our language can also give us a massive clue. Phrases such as:

part of me

yes, but

on the one hand

all indicate a level of internal incongruence.

You can, of course, choose to ignore your own incongruence but, if you do, you won't have an achievable outcome.

When you've worked through these six conditions, using the insights you gained in the previous two chapters, you'll be a lot closer both to knowing what your outcome is and to being clear about what you and others have to do to make it a reality. If you're still with the kids in the back of the car and aren't quite there yet, use the TOTE model we met in part I (see chapter III) and recycle through whatever you need to until you are.

Once you're absolutely sure what your outcome is, you can move into the strategic planning stage. Design yourself an action plan, ensuring that it includes at least one step that you can take immediately. You may know what your outcome is, but you still have to work to bring it into being.

Chapter XIV

Getting our strategies straight

PDJ

If what we're doing isn't working,

let's do something different.

Now that we know where we're heading in general terms at least, if not in the fine detail, it's time to think about the strategies we'll be using to reach our destination. We all have mental strategies in place already; we just might not be accustomed to calling them that. As our PDJ highlights so succinctly, not all of them are fit for purpose. I'll tell you about two of mine: one is an outright winner; the other a downright loser.

Many moons ago when I were a young girl in the London suburbs, I had a Sunday paper round. The papers were so heavy that the wicker basket on the front of my bike bowed and groaned under the weight. The dawn start could be daunting, so I used to chant to myself:

One more is one less.

That chant got me all the way round from 73 Palmerston Road to 54 Wayside and the point at which I could finally mount and ride my bike for the remainder of the round. By the time I returned to the newsagents, I was riding on air. Some Sundays, my mood was dashed by the disappointing news that my brother had failed to get out of bed. With family honour at stake, I would have to do his round as well, but that's another story. The point is that I'd unconsciously developed a really successful strategy.

Not all of mine were that good. I had a repeating pattern of ordering a meal in a restaurant, looking at said meal when it turned up and declaring:

That's not what I ordered.

My dining companions would fall about laughing and insist that it was. Before I became initiated into the mysteries of NLP, I had absolutely no idea why there was such a mis-match between what I thought I'd ordered and what the waiter brought me.

Post-NLP learning, the penny dropped. I was using my visual rep system to design my meal in great detail, exactly the way I would have cooked and presented it. My meal had become so real in my map of the world that when chef's version of it landed in front of me it was completely unrecognizable. I went straight into denial.

Once I realized that my strategy wasn't fit for purpose because it delivered disappointment rather than delight, I changed it completely. These days, when I order a meal, I give my highly-developed visual sense a wide berth and go directly to my kinaesthetic. I ask myself:

What do I feel like eating?

Edible pleasure guaranteed; it works every time.

A surprising number of us run unsuccessful strategies repeatedly as I used to do in restaurants, without ever stopping to consider either what's really going on or how we could change them for the better.

One of the most prevalent unsuccessful strategies we use is disaster scenario planning. I'm not talking about this in the context of corporate life with emergency telephone numbers and cascading contact details in the event of fire, flood, terrorism, and other unlikely eventualities, but in the context of our own internal system.

Even if we're already acknowledging that we're in transition, even if we're cutting ourselves enough slack, even if we're giving ourselves permission to have a bad day if we're so inclined, we can still get completely wrapped up in this insidious strategy.

I have to admit that it's not a strategy I adopt very often but, probably as an offshoot of the synchronicity that seems to pervade my life at the moment, I did put myself through a stonkingly good example of it the other day.

I was in the kitchen doing the washing up when I noticed that a fat food ball that I'd put out for the birds had moved from where I'd hung it to the back fence. It registered, but I didn't pay that much attention, having other things on my mind. I went back upstairs to my study; when I came down to the kitchen two hours later to make some coffee, the food ball had disappeared completely. I was beginning to feel uneasy, but I kept my feelings in check.

On reaching my study, the phone rang. I answered; there was no-one on the other end. That was it: I was off. Fuelled by all the recent reporting on BBC Radio Four's *Yesterday in Parliament* about the new law on stalking, my mind knew that I was in clear and present danger.

Someone's been in my garden; that someone is guilty of theft and trespass.

What should I do first? Go to the police station or call in at the locksmiths?

I'm supposed to be going out tonight? Should I still go? If I do go, I must take my valuables with me, and when I get back I need to get the heavy-duty wrench out of the cupboard under the sink and take it up to my bedroom with me.

You'll have noticed just how many modal operators of necessity I had in play here. Those are just the edited highlights; I won't bore you with the rest. It wasn't until I said:

Whoa!

to myself that I was able to stop the images, voices and feelings that had taken over control of my entire system. And I didn't return wholeheartedly to planet sanity until I'd asked and answered the question:

What do I actually know as a fact?

This proved to be a surprisingly small tally: one food ball had first moved and then disappeared. Back in the realm of the rational, I realized that this could have been either a magpie or a squirrel at work, and I consequently didn't need either to pop into the police station where they'd probably have pigeon-holed me as the local lunatic or spend my hard-earned cash on a new alarm system.

Phew, that's a relief!

While I was in it though, it all seemed real, reasonable and rational in the extreme. If you're prone to this type of strategy, you've probably become very good at it. You might not have deconstructed it though – to see how you do what you do. There are three elements to this; pay attention to:

- the rep systems you're using;

- the submodalities you're using; and

- the sequence in which you do things.

In my example, I was using all three rep systems, thereby ensuring that, as well as having an unpleasant experience, I was having the most vividly unpleasant experience possible. My visual submodalities were big, bright, moving pictures up close and personal; auditory ones included doom-laden critical voices all round my head. Just to complete this sensory smorgasbord, I also had those nausea-inducing feelings in the pit of my stomach that I get when I feel that I'm not in control of anything.

As we learned in chapter VI, we can change our submodalities at will. Doing this will change our state which makes it much easier to change our strategy. You can also do what I did which is to add into the sequence what I've decided to call a dead man's switch.

Wisegeek.com tells me that a dead man's switch turns a system off when the operator experiences a problem, becomes incapacitated, harassed or disrupted. Sounds perfect for our purposes. My dead man's switch consisted of some internal dialogue: command + question + answer.

You can construct yourself a dead man's switch in whatever rep system works best for you. I have one client who has a large red and white STOP sign that flips up in his visual field whenever he feels himself going into disaster scenario planning. Another musically gifted client whose auditory system is dominant hears The Supremes singing 'Stop! In the Name of Love!', followed by their legendary gesture of one hand on hip and the other outstretched in a STOP gesture as a visual back-up.

My foray into disaster scenario planning was an isolated incident, but people who do this habitually can make themselves feel really bad with saddening regularity. Danny, one of my younger clients, had spent so much time imagining all the things that could possibly go wrong during a business trip that he didn't have room in his head for anything else. He only realized this when a friend asked him if he wanted to play tennis the week after the trip.

I had to tell him that I'd get back to him. The block in my head was so huge that I couldn't see past it. I couldn't imagine surviving the business trip and having a life afterwards.

Just read those words again and notice how debilitating they are. Danny had disabled his lead rep system so effectively that he was stuck in a completely unresourceful state. What was particularly interesting was that Danny knew exactly what was going on in his internal experience; knew too that he couldn't quell it by willpower alone. The one thing he didn't know was how to fix it.

I showed Danny how to change his state and build himself a positive, resourceful strategy. When we understand our strategies, we begin to understand the driving force behind them. Armed with this information, we can then decide whether to change our strategy or not. What's even better, we can keep on refining it until it works perfectly for us.

Farida, one of my corporate clients, is a great example of this. She kept failing her professional exams. Although Farida was outstandingly good at her job, she couldn't pursue the career path she wanted without exam success. She was becoming increasingly frustrated as she saw those who were less talented, less experienced, and younger overtake her on the career ladder.

When we deconstructed what was going on in the exam room, we discovered that Farida had created an automatic association in her memory between stress and the worst experience of her life to date: when her father cast her out of her family because she chose to marry against his wishes.

We changed the machine code of that memory in much the same way as Tom and I did in chapter IX. After Farida had future paced her next session in the exam room, I asked her:

How could you make this even better?

Her reply came back instantly:

*Instead of telling myself that I've **only** got ten minutes, I'm going to tell myself that I've got a **whole** ten minutes.'*

This demonstrates yet again the importance of the language we use to ourselves. The word *only* put Farida under immense pressure.

Quick, quick, I've got to work out what my answer is, think of the best way of expressing it, and get it down on paper – all in ten minutes.

The word *whole*, on the other hand, led her into a completely different, more relaxed experience.

OK, I've got a whole ten minutes to answer this. All I've got to do is gather my thoughts together, assemble them in a logical order, and pop them down on paper.

By changing one word in her internal dialogue, Farida completely reframed her approach to answering exam questions. With a successful strategy in place, she passed all of her remaining exams in one go.

One of the most important ways in which we can use strategies in our current circumstances is in the context of motivation. Without the daily routine imposed on us by the necessity of having to get up and go to work, it can sometimes be quite difficult to motivate ourselves to do anything at all.

Martin, one of my first ever coaching clients, used to find it really difficult to motivate himself to begin any task that involved making a phone call to a client. Given that he worked in a client team and had ambitions to go far in the corporate world, this was something of a self-sabotaging strategy.

Elaine: *So what's the first thing you do when you know you have to call a client.*

Martin: *Add it to my to do list.*

Elaine: *Then what?*

Martin: *I look at it and it looks horrible, so I look at all the other things on the list that are more attractive and do those instead, striking them through as I go.*

Elaine: *What happens next?*

Martin: *The phone call starts to look isolated, so I ink over it to make it bolder so that I can't ignore it, but all that does is make it look even worse.*

Elaine: *So you're even less inclined to do it?*

Martin: *Well, yes, but that's when the voices start.*

Elaine: *The voices?*

Martin: *The voices that scream and shout at me, pointing out that if I don't make the phone call sometime soon, the consequences will be dire.*

Elaine: *Is that the point at which you finally make the call?*

Martin: *Yes.*

When the two of us unpicked this, we found out that the very first thing Martin did when he knew he had to call a client – even before he added it to his to do list – was to see and hear it going very badly wrong, even though he had no hard evidence to prove that this would be the case in reality. This was an example of disaster scenario planning in disguise.

The crunch point came when he really did have to make a sensitive phone call to a client – and he had to do it that day. He came to see me in a complete panic.

Martin: *This is absolutely the worst thing that could have happened. I've sent a client a report telling her one thing, and now a director's phoned her – without reference to me – and told her something different. She's going to be fuming.*

Elaine: *How do you know?*

Martin: *Well, it's not great is it? She's paying us for professional advice, and we've given her two different opinions.*

Elaine: *Isn't there usually room for interpretation?*

Martin: *Yes, I suppose there is.*

Elaine: *So how can you reframe what you're about to tell her? Can you reframe it in a positive rather than a negative light?*

Martin realized that he could do this very easily, without compromising either himself, the director or the company. We role-played the conversation a couple of times, and then Martin mentally rehearsed it by future pacing.

I waited while he went back to his office to make the call. When he returned, he was beaming broadly. It had gone so well that by the time the client had put the phone down she'd already commissioned Martin to do some additional work for her. She was delighted that he'd taken so much care and paid so much attention.

Using the insights he gained from this experience, Martin has now designed himself a completely different strategy for phone calls that involves positive images, voices and feelings, rather than negative ones. Now it's not just clients he can call with ease; he regularly speaks to journalists on the phone as well.

Before we leave this topic, I'll just introduce you to a little exercise that can be invaluable when you want to change your behaviour. It's an elegantly effective combo of role modelling and future pacing called the new behaviour generator.

1 Identify the role model with the behaviour you want for yourself.

2 Close your eyes and imagine you're watching a short film of that person doing whatever it is that you want to model. Notice all aspects of their physiology, including body posture, movement and breathing, how they interact with the external world, and how and what they communicate.

3 Now run the film again, but this time put yourself in your role model's place.

4 Make sure you that you feel completely comfortable in this role. If you don't feel 100% congruent, change one thing (eg body posture, breathing) at a time until you do.

5 Associate into the picture completely so that you're looking out through your own eyes.

6 Talk to yourself about what it's like to be this person with these new behavioural abilities.

7 Think of a situation in the future where you want to have these abilities.

8 Imagine yourself in that situation behaving in that way.

9 Associate into the picture completely so that you're looking out through your own eyes.

10 Make any necessary adjustments.

11 Come back to the present.

12 Practise being yourself with these new behaviours by walking around and noticing how it feels. If you want, you can anchor the feeling in some way (see chapter III).

13 Adopt the new behaviour as soon as you possibly can. It won't be long before it becomes second nature.

Using what you already know about NLP, you can create yourself a successful strategy for whatever's on the horizon – job interviews, networking sessions, appointments with professional advisers – using anything we've covered so far: states, resources, role models, timelines – in any combination you like.

Chapter XV

Building more rapport

> ## PDJ
>
> *Rapport is meeting individuals
> in their map of the world.*

And so we come to the last of the four pillars of NLP which is arguably also the most powerful. One on-line dictionary[32] defines rapport as:

a close and harmonious relationship in which the people or groups concerned understand each other's feelings or ideas and communicate well.

I really don't think I can improve on that. If you want to see rapport in the raw, then pay attention the next time you're in a restaurant and notice what's going on at those tables where harmony reigns supreme. The people will seem to be engaging in a very natural ebb and flow of energy and rhythm in which all parties are acknowledged and valued and which appears to be completely self-regulating. How do they do that?

We need to know because rapport is the basis of effective communication and that's a skill that we need in spades as we deal with the transition into the next phase of our life. You will, of course, encounter some people with whom you are naturally in rapport. The skills I'm addressing here are for when that isn't the case.

I like to think of rapport as the keystone of NLP because it involves the use of all three of the other fundamental principles:

- sensory acuity – to sense, feel and hear what's important for the other person or people;

- outcome orientation – to be aware of your purpose in communicating and to know what you want out of it; and

- behavioural flexibility – to act in such a way that you meet others in their map of the world.

We've already met some of the concepts that are going to help us to build more rapport and to become an even more effective communicator than we already are. Before we re-engage with those, let's get acquainted with some new ones.

If we revert to our example of harmonious people in a restaurant, you'll probably notice an astonishing degree of mirroring between people in rapport: their posture, gestures, speed and tonality of speech, level of energy, even their breathing can match. The next time you're with someone with whom you have natural rapport, set yourself the task of noticing just how often your bodies match in this way.

Mirroring some aspects of another person's body language is a very respectful – and effective – way of building rapport because the intention behind it is to share the other person's experience by venturing into it. Rapport is a subtle and elusive creature, so remember to respond in kind by being subtle. Match the other person's posture, frequency of eye contact, voice tone and speed by all means, but do not mimic them. Mimicry is nothing more than a thinly veiled form of mockery, and is more likely to provoke a punch on the nose than enhanced rapport.

As we discovered in chapter IV, language can give us a huge clue as to people's preferred rep system. The precise words that people use are very important for them; also for us if we want to establish and build rapport with them. Paraphrasing what people say does not acknowledge their message in the same way as actually using their own words. It may even make the speaker feel that you have failed to understand their exact meaning.

I'm not asking you to role model Polly the proverbial parrot here; parroting someone's words back to them will have the opposite effect of the one you want. However, if you use your sensory acuity to notice which words are particularly important to the other person, which ones they are marking out by their use of tone, and use those same words, then the person will understand not only that you have heard and understood the message, but also that you respect both message and speaker.

Understanding which rep system someone is using can give you a head start in terms of enhancing your rapport with them because you'll know in advance how they take in and process information. If we don't have this information, it can sometimes be difficult to communicate with those who use a different system. We can end up at odds with one another without realizing quite why or how.

When I was still in corporate life and before I knew about rep systems, I had to write an executive summary for one of the partners. He called me into his office to discuss my first attempt.

Dennis: *This doesn't feel right.*

Elaine: (out loud) *OK, what would you like to see instead?*

Elaine: (to herself) *?!? How can it not feel right? It's a piece of paper with words on it. Not sound right – yes, I get that. Not look right – if he doesn't like the layout, yes, but how on earth can it not feel right?*

Dennis: *I need to feel that this is going to appeal directly to the client, that he'll read it and know in his heart of hearts that he wants to work with us.*

Elaine: (to herself) *It's an executive summary; not the Sermon on the Mount. What's this guy on?*

Elaine: (out loud) *You'd like to see a second version then?*

Dennis: *Yes, please.*

Elaine: *Can you give me more of a perspective on the changes you'd like to see?*

Dennis: *Not really.*

I left the meeting feeling really frustrated and I rather suspect that Dennis felt the same. There'd been an undercurrent of tension because, at some level, we both knew that we were miscommunicating. Fortunately, the following weekend, I went to a one-day NLP workshop and fell upon rep systems as a hungry wolf upon a lamb.

Remembering just how often Dennis had referred to his feelings, I realized that he was kinaesthetic. That's why he hadn't responded well to my visual language. I did have to tinker with the executive summary – not because the carefully crafted messages were wrong, but because I'd couched them in the wrong language for Dennis. It would, of course, have been altogether more sensible to write the piece in the language most likely to appeal to the reader – the potential client – but there's only so much one can achieve in any one corporate lifetime.

When I took the revised summary back to Dennis, I strolled confidently into his office and kicked off with:

How does it feel to you this time?

We were away: both of us on the same track.

Being aware of these subtleties is a really useful skill. Jason, one of my friends, is a past master at translating across rep systems. It's a skill he learned early on because of the sensory bias of his parents. Although they love one another dearly, mutual communication has never been a strong point. Jason's mother is kinaesthetic; his father is visual; Jason is a combination of the two. He spent his childhood being their translator; he's spending his adulthood being everyone else's.

There isn't an exact job-title for what Jason does, but he's already had two successful careers – in the rag trade and in television – and he's now reinventing himself as an entrepreneur. In his business life, he's something of a Mr Fix-It, the go-to person when things need a kick up the bum to get started and keep moving. His abilities spill over into his social life as well. The other week, there was a bit of a hoo-ha at his local swimming pool. The serious swimmers were at loggerheads with management over the lane allocation.

Almost before Jason knew what was happening, he found himself elected as the swimmers' representative, delegated to go to a management meeting to get it all sorted. Respected by those on both sides of the divide because of his rapport-building skills, Jason was able to lead the way to an allocation that met with everyone's approval. I've used the word *lead* advisedly because I just want to mention pacing and leading which is another important element of rapport.

The analogy here relates to walking, to matching your pace to someone else's. It's an outstandingly good analogy because it emphasises the fact that, having established rapport with someone, you're now both in the same model of the world and can harmoniously arrive at the same place at the same time. In terms of effective communication, that's absolutely priceless.

Claire, an ex-colleague, uses rep systems and pacing and leading together to stunningly good effect. Once she's sussed out which system you use, she asks you, at appropriate intervals during the conversation:

how does that look/sound/feel to you?

Occasionally, she asks:

Are you with me?

I only know this is how Claire does what she does so well because I used her as a role model. I was intrigued by the way she made me feel during our conversations: not just listened to and acknowledged, but honoured at a very deep level.

Rapport also involves one other really important concept: chunk size. If you've previously only ever associated those two words with cat and dog food, please think again.

We all run various types of meta programmes (also known as sorting principles). For instance, some of us move towards what we want; some us move away from what we don't want. Some of us focus primarily on ourselves; some of us focus primarily on others. In the case we're discussing here, some of us chunk down into specifics; some of us chunk up into generalities.

If we chunk down, then we tend to perceive tasks in terms of their individual parts, need to have all the details and specific examples to hand, and have to understand the sequence of steps involved before we begin.

If we chunk up, we tend to perceive tasks in terms of their overall concept and direction, need to understand the bigger picture and abstract examples before we can address the individual elements, and find step-by-step procedures frustrating.

As with so much else in NLP, what we're discussing here are our preferences. We're all capable of chunking in both directions. However, if you understand another person's preference, communication becomes a lot easier. Here's an illuminating example from my corporate coaching practice.

Elizabeth was responsible for drafting an employee handbook on behalf of her HR director. She habitually chunked down, so every time the handbook went through yet another set of revisions, she felt duty bound to give the HR director a blow-by-blow account of all the editorial changes: who'd done what, when, how and why.

Unfortunately, the HR director chunked up so Elizabeth's meticulously compiled reports overwhelmed her to such an extent that she'd be in enraged bull mode even before the meeting started.

Elizabeth was at a loss to understand what was going on, even when the HR director screamed at her:

Will you please just give me the sodding headlines?

When Elizabeth understood that she was presenting the information in a way that made it almost impossible for the HR director to receive it, she also understood that she was unlikely to achieve her outcome of getting sign-off from the HR director until she changed her communication style. What had seemed like a dereliction of duty in her map of the world became a path to effective communication in the HR director's.

We do a lot of this rapport stuff naturally. For example, I have a couple of friends who are decidedly and distinctly top-drawer. I've noticed that in their company my voice becomes posher. Conversely, when I'm joshing with the lads on the stalls in the veg market, my voice becomes even more sowf London than usual. I'm not doing it deliberately; it just happens and is usually out of my conscious awareness.

The last thing I want to do is make you self-conscious about what you're already doing so well. What I do want to do though is to make you aware that building rapport is a skill that can be learned and refined so that we can all have more rapport with more people more often when it's useful.

Before we leave this fascinating topic, I'd just like to remind all of us that rapport has an internal, intimate dimension. Our conscious and unconscious minds can be in rapport with one another or not, known as congruence and incongruence, as discussed in chapter XIII.

Chapter XVI

Perfecting our plasticity

PDJ

What's possible for one person is possible for anyone.
It's only a matter of how.

As we near the end of this part of the book, I'm going to refer back to the *Horizon* programme that I watched in March 2012.[33] One of the most interesting things about it for me was the fact that science has finally caught up with what the coaching world has known for decades: the brain can re-wire itself by creating new neural pathways. The scientific term for this is plasticity.

I saw a wonderful example of this in a coaching session the other day. One of my redundancy clients has a new job (hooray, hooray). As is often the case, he was being thrown in at the deep end. Do turn up on your first day and be pitched head first into a four-hour quarterly client review meeting, even though you don't know anybody on either side of the table.

He was understandably nervous, so we spent some time talking through the issues, agreeing what outcome he wanted and the resources he would need. He was keen to strike the right balance between contributing something worthwhile to the discussion so that he didn't appear to be a non-speaking extra and not making an idiot of himself because of his lack of knowledge.

At the end of the meeting, he sent me a text:

…the best thing is that I noticed on a few occasions that the old ways were trying to creep in but I managed to spot it and keep focused and be open to what the new team was saying. I even gave them a few thoughts worth thinking about (as they put it)…

This is an amazing tribute to the power of the unconscious. Not only are the new neural pathways already in place, enabling my client to behave in a new and completely different way, but he's already labelled his previous behaviour as *the old ways*.

I don't have any scientific evidence for this but I think, based on my own experience, that there's a beautiful balance between creation and extinction at work here. As we create new neural pathways, old and unhelpful ones wither and die. Here's an example that doesn't show me in a very good light, but I've already shared so much with you that I may as well be up front here as well.

A while back, a family member annoyed me to such an extent that I decided to leave behind everything I know about rapport, outcome orientation, behavioural flexibility, the whole shebang. I just wanted to punish him.

What did I used to do in these circumstances? Oh yes, I used to go into a sullen and sulky tantrum worthy of a six-year old and not talk to him for several hours. That's what I'll do now.

I spent a good ten minutes trying to work myself up into a tantrum before I was prepared to admit that it wasn't going to happen. Tantrums don't appear to be part of my personal behavioural repertoire any longer.

If I'd persisted, I could probably have got there; we're only talking about a state after all, and we all know by now that we can access any state we want. I didn't persist though, because bluntly what was the point? Much saner, safer and more sensible to feel grateful that the neural pathway that led directly to tantrum mode was so overgrown that it had fallen into disuse. I donned the motley of behavioural flexibility and domestic harmony reigned again.

Knowing that we can reshape ourselves and our lives using any or all of the techniques outlined in this book can make a huge difference to us as we work our way towards our new niche in life. Recognize too that it's OK to take baby steps (yes, we're back with our role model of the toddler again), to be uncertain about our precise destination, and to be confused.

Nothing wrong with being confused – not all of the time, obviously – but confusion is actually the gateway to understanding. As children, we used to be confused about loads of stuff – shoelaces and ties, to name but two particularly knotty examples, but we got over it. Unless we hail from an extremely elevated social milieu, we can all now tie our own shoelaces and knot our own tie.

Nothing wrong either with not knowing how to do something. I didn't know how to write a book, Naomi didn't know how to put on a musical (see part IV); Cathy tells me that she keeps volunteering for things that she doesn't know how to do (see part IV). Our ignorance didn't stop any of us – and yours doesn't need to stop you.

Life's a learning process and learning any new skill entails a progression from unconscious incompetence through to unconscious competence. Just reflect for a moment on your experience of learning to play a musical instrument or drive a car.

When we're at the level of unconscious incompetence, we're blissfully ignorant. We don't know that we don't know. Once we've made it up the ladder to the second level of conscious incompetence, we know that we don't know. One level up, we've clawed our way to conscious competence. We know that we know – even if we still have to practise and concentrate. By the time we get to level four (unconscious competence), we don't know that we know because our performance has become automatic and easy.

Whatever our future plans may be, here's a couple of things to ponder. There's a concept in NLP called logical levels; the levels in question are:

- identity (who?);

- beliefs and values (why?);

- capability (how?);

- behaviour (what?); and

- environment (where/when?).

Let's use a simple example to see how the levels work in practice. Imagine that you're considering working from home as a freelance professional of some kind. If you were in a negative frame of mind, you could say to yourself:

I can't earn money doing that at home.

In this case, the equation works out like this:

I = identity

can't = belief

earn money doing = capability

that = behaviour

at home = environment.

By breaking it down like this, it's much easier to see where the discomfort or incongruence, if any, lies. Are you unhappy at the thought of inviting clients into your home? If so, it's an environmental issue. Is it the thought of exercising your profession that's bothering you? This relates to behaviour. Or does being a professional practitioner clash with your sense of who you are? In this case, it's an identity issue.

Once we know which level is causing the problem, we know where we need to intervene and change things. We are, of course, a complete system all by ourselves so, when we change something on one level, there'll often be a commensurate change on the others as well.

Just so you know, some NLP models have a sixth logical level known as beyond identify or spiritual self. This is deemed to be a higher level of experience in which we have stepped fully into ourselves and our life's purpose. Personally, I'm all for it; I just feel that right now we have more than enough on our plate working out what it is that we want to do after our encounter with the axe-wielding flunkies.

The second thing I want you to consider is feedback; in my map of the world, feedback lives right next door to the logical levels. Notice if you will how differently you respond to these two statements:

You're too abrupt.

Sometimes, you can respond rather too abruptly.

The first one's like a smack in the face because it's about who we are; it goes straight to the sacred place that is our identity. The second one is much more palatable because it's about what we do: our behaviour. As we all know by now, we are not our behaviour. Just why so many managers continue to give us feedback as if we are what we do will have to remain one of life's mysteries, right up there with the Bermuda Triangle, the Mary Celeste, and the Lost City of Atlantis.

Mercifully, my topic here isn't the feedback sandwich so beloved of corporate organizations – the one with the bad news in the middle like a leaf of limp lettuce. While we're thinking about that though, let's acknowledge its role in making us slightly detached from the act of receiving feedback. We so don't want to hear the bad news that we dissociate from the good as well. One year at work, someone wrote this about me:

Elaine is an entertaining and persuasive public speaker.

At that point in my life, I was so detached from all my feedback that I unconsciously edited out the first word. I thought the statement related to one of the people I managed; it was only when she pointed out that the sentence began with my name that I realized my mistake.

There's a lesson for us all here: when you get positive feedback, associate into it; if you get negative feedback, dissociate out of it (go back to chapter VI for an explanation of the difference). If we brush off positive feedback, not only are we disregarding high quality information that could be really useful as we find our new niche in life, we're also denying ourselves well-deserved acknowledgement. So do take it personally; associate so deeply that you're positively revelling in it.

One Saturday, I was manning our vintage toy stall in the Portobello Road Antique Market. I was dealing with a particularly exacting group of doll collectors from the Netherlands. They had every right to be exacting: they were the customers. They wanted to see most of the dolls on display on the high shelves, so I had to climb up and down the ladder, clinging precariously to the stall structure with one hand and cradling precious antique dolls in the other. With both feet back on terra firma, I started enthusing about the merchandise.

To appreciate the sub-text of this story, you need to understand two things about me. One, in common with all dyspraxic individuals, I can be clumsy and accident-prone. Two, I have a dislike of dolls dating back to childhood. Imagine how supremely annoying it was to be given a walking, talking doll when all I craved was a Dan Dare walkie-talkie interplanetary space set.

Anyway, back to the toy stall. After extensive negotiating, I sold a lot of dolls and the collectors went home happy. My father – who had been watching, but not intervening because he saw that I'd established rapport with the customers – winked at me, smiled, and said:

you were majestic.

Did I take that personally? Yes. Did it make me feel like a million dollars? Yes. Does it still have the power to make me feel that way? Yes. Have I added it to my library of states so that I can re-access it at any time I like? Too damn right I have.

Even if you get negative feedback, it's still useful information that can teach you something – as long as you remember to dissociate from it so that you can look back at it from a distance.

Time for Eeyore's second appearance in this book. He may be the *old grey Donkey;* he may be pessimistic and subject to bouts of persecution mania; but he's also remarkably perspicacious. In one film[34], he says:

Days, weeks, months, who knows?

This is precisely what's wrong with formal feedback. We never quite know when we're going to get it; usually, by the time we do, we've forgotten the original stimulus. Just let your mind drift back to tests at school.

The key to making feedback work for us is to use our sensory acuity to notice how people are responding to us in the here and now, and then refine our behaviour based on that instantaneous information until we get the outcome we want.

As usual, there's a PDJ for accompaniment:

there's no such thing as failure, only feedback. We can use every experience.

Remember Petr from chapter IV? After he'd made the acquaintance of the meta-mirror (also in chapter IV), I introduced him to the concept of feedback as nothing more than information. He'd just finished a riff on how he'd never been given any decent feedback because the people giving it weren't qualified to do so and always had their own axe to grind anyway.

Petr: *It's just information?*

Elaine: *Yes, just information; but information that could be useful to you.*

Petr: *Information that could be useful to me?*

Elaine: *In the sense that it could highlight things that you might want to change or improve – regardless of the inadequacies of the system or of the people involved.*

Petr: *I've never thought about it like this.*

Thinking about it like this clearly had a huge impact on Petr's life: he's developed what I can only describe as antennae. He's become so attuned to other people that it's almost as if he can see their thought processes. He's now so adept at reading others that he can spot problems, objections and resistance way ahead of time. Petr starts formulating his response and potential solutions before anyone else in the room even realizes that there's something amiss.

Learning to receive feedback as just information affected me massively as well because it sparked my commitment to personal development. I speak as someone who has a history of being very, very afraid of feedback. I used to have to steel myself for at least 72 hours before I could open any of the wretched stuff. Now I absolutely love it. How did this happen?

Well, it all started one year in the office, during the annual appraisal round. That particular year, most of my feedback was harsh – and some it was delivered harshly as well – but at least two people had my best interests at heart. The way in which they expressed their feedback made all the difference. Although it forced me to confront some unpleasant truths about my behaviour, it also brought me to the realization that there was another way of doing things. I didn't always have to be in defensive mode; I didn't always have to beat myself up when things went wrong.

There's one other really valuable thing I've learned about feedback, and I didn't learn it on a course or from a book. I learned it from friend John – which, as an aside, just goes to show how much we can learn from the wisdom of others if we're open to it.

I've now turned what John taught me into a really useful habit. Here's how it goes. After any experience – good, bad or indifferent – ask yourself:

What have I learned from that?

It means that you pay attention both to those things you're doing really well – which, as we discussed in chapter VII, can only build your self-esteem – and to those things where there's still room for improvement. We're all work in progress, so all we're doing here is gathering useful information as we move from our present state to our desired state.

Sometimes we automatically assume that personal change has to be difficult and protracted; it doesn't. When I was learning to be a coach, I had to experience life on both sides of the coaching relationship: as coach and client. When I was deciding what to tackle as the client, I determined that I wasn't going to go anywhere near my relationship with my mother, even though I knew it was probably the biggest issue in my life.

That determination lasted a whole five minutes into my first session. It came to an abrupt end when I realized that everything I wanted to change about myself stemmed from that relationship. I now know – with absolute certainty – that my mother was doing the very best she could for all of us. She had such an unpromising start in life that I'm genuinely amazed that she achieved as much as she did. She didn't set out to erode my self-confidence or make me feel negative about myself, but the law of unintended consequences came into play and her best intentions for me went badly awry.

I'd always thought that I'd lack the courage to tackle all that negativity and that, even if I found the courage from somewhere, it would be a dreadfully upsetting experience. I didn't and it wasn't. It was surprisingly easy. I came out of the coaching not just as my own person, but with a much more positive attitude towards my mother. I also realized for the first time just how much energy I'd been devoting to suppressing everything.

At the beginning of this book, I told you that we were going to be working with two of the most powerful forces known to mankind: memory and imagination. Our memories – of ourselves and of others – are precious as well as powerful. They can inspire us to action and remind us of those times when we've had a glimpse of just how uniquely authentic and amazing we can be when we show up in our own lives.

I often have a thought in my head about the past being a point of reference rather than a place to hang out. I haven't been able to trace its origin; perhaps it's in my head because that's where it germinated; doesn't matter. What does matter is that we recognize the difference between being shaped by our past and letting our past shape our future.

Yes, redundancy can suck, but it can also be an important turning point in our life. The stories in part IV of this book demonstrate just how true that can be. Without redundancy, I'd never have had the glorious experience of writing a book – finally, after nearly 40 years of dreaming. More importantly though, I'd never have found my own authentic voice.

Let's end this self-help part of the book with a tribute to that awe-inspiring gift that we all possess: imagination. Just to put it in context, here's what Albert Einstein said about it:

Imagination is more important than knowledge.

I don't know how the dictionary defines imagination and, for once, I'm not going to look. I'm going to define it here as the power to believe that things could be other than they are, to see/feel/hear that difference and then start to make it a reality.

Charles F Kettering, an American inventor, engineer, businessman, holder of no fewer than 186 patents, and best known today for the introduction of the electrical starter motor and leaded petrol, expressed it more eloquently:

Our imagination is the only limit to what we can hope to have in the future.

Here's hoping.

Part III

Professional Perspectives

Chapter XVII

Why is redundancy so often conducted in a less than ideal manner?

Annabel Kaye is an employment law specialist I met through Twitter. She's been involved in employment law since it came into being in the 1970s. She worked in HR or personnel, as it was then. Today, 60% of her business relates to employers and 40% to employees, so Annabel knows about both sides of redundancy. I ask her for her views.

Her starting point is that the law on redundancy really isn't complicated, despite everything you hear to the contrary.

If a business employs five people, but can only afford four, what's complicated about that?

She does admit, however, that there's a bewildering array of case law which has come into being mainly because redundancy appeared on the scene in the 1960s (redundancy payments existed before unfair dismissal).

From the 60s onwards, people have been arguing about the ins and outs of redundancy to such an extent that we can now debate the case law in much the same way that mediaeval scholars used to debate how many angels could sit on a pin head.

Annabel wants me to understand the three legal definitions that lie behind redundancy:

- the workplace disappears;

- the work either reduces or diminishes, or is expected to do so;

- the need of a business for employees to undertake work of a particular kind has either ceased or diminished, or is expected to do so.

Sometimes, it's a genuine restructuring; sometimes it's the need to save money. In the latter case, it's often a question of contracts. Ending the lease on the bosses' cars isn't actually going to make that much difference since usually the payments still have to be made. Sometimes, it's easier to get out of staff contracts than it is to terminate the lease for the photocopier.

This can lead to the 'extra insanity', as Annabel calls it, of bosses turning up in their brand new XJS luxury cars on the same day as a company is making 100 employees redundant (see Rebecca's story in part IV).

Annabel is adamant that, if employers want to make the best fist they can of redundancy, they need to follow three golden rules:

1 decide the scale and scope of the job cuts;

2 establish what method they're going to use and implement it fairly and objectively; and

3 consider what, when, how and to whom they're going to communicate, taking into account those employees who for one reason or another (sick leave, holidays, maternity/paternity leave) will be absent on announcement day.

It's the comms piece that is key to doing redundancies well, and that's the piece that's missing most often. Communication in redundancy now exists solely at the level of 'What do we need to do to ensure that we don't get sued?'. It's the Trade Descriptions Act approach to redundancy. Compliance has done away with dignity, compassion and humanity.

Over the years she's been in practice, Annabel's come to the conclusion that there are three classes of redundancy: strategic, middle eight, and crisis.

Strategic: every organization conducts these fairly regularly. They occur when a company is either restructuring or moving out of a specific market or location, and has no further need of various high-earners. The redundancies are well thought out, delivered well, and often include a generous compromise agreement and outplacement arrangements.

They involve minimum consultation so employers focus on modelling the package rather than the communication. Those being made redundant are initially shocked and disappointed, but recover relatively quickly because of the size and nature of the package. Unfortunately, this strategic approach becomes the model for everyone else.

Middle eight: organizations conduct these in order to facilitate the business doing what it does to make money. Those leaving are reasonably well compensated; they tend to have a sense of entitlement because they know the size of the usual 'strategic' package via the organizational grapevine. However, they can often feel badly treated because of the absence of any meaningful level of communication.

Crisis: these occur when organizations don't have enough money for their payroll obligations next month. Employees are lucky if they get paid at all, and consultation and communication are reduced to a bare minimum.

Compulsory collective consultation with elected representatives enters the equation when employers want to avoid successful unfair dismissal claims being made against them. If they're considering making 20 or more employees redundant, a 30-day consultation period is mandatory, increasing to 90 days if 100 or more staff are at risk. Annabel's experience demonstrates that this consultation process is often just as much of a problem as the redundancies themselves.

She draws an interesting analogy between redundancy consultation and launching a new product.

If you had a manufacturing company and had developed a new product, you'd spend significant time and money putting together a promotional and marketing campaign and identifying and segmenting your audience. Currently, the government is considering reducing the collective redundancy consultation period from 90 to 60 days. Unless you're a communications genius, your chances of doing it well in that time frame are remote.

Annabel takes the view that frogmarching employees off the premises with their personal possessions in a cardboard box, and telling them to go home for 90 days and not contact anyone at work is rarely necessary.

There are some circumstances when employers do have to isolate people. If employees have access to sensitive information, in the financial services sector for example, that can be a security risk to the business. *But human beings are herd animals at heart; when animals in the wild are shunned and isolated, they're being abandoned and left to die.*

Annabel believes that there's a much better way, that employers can do a lot – most of it relatively inexpensively – during the consultation period days, to demonstrate that they understand the employee perspective.

Given that 60% of jobs in this country are never advertised and that people who've been in post for 20 years aren't going to have the faintest idea how to get a job, providing outplacement and CV advice can be really valuable. This is the polar opposite of just telling people to phone the employee assistance helpline which won't be able to help anyway.

In Annabel's experience, getting the consultation process right involves segmenting those employees potentially at risk into groups, dealing with each group one at a time, and explaining exactly what's happening. With this approach, employees don't mind waiting. If, for instance, an employer manages to reduce the number of employees at risk from 400 to 350 through natural wastage, then there's good news to report.

When nothing happens, employees do feel as if the sword of Damocles is hanging over them because they're in a state of total uncertainty. Often, they'd rather opt for the certainty of a brutal redundancy process than the continuing uncertainty. That can seem like a fair swap.

Annabel then dissects and analyzes the role that the HR professional and the manager play in a typical redundancy meeting. She begins with a diverting and interesting take on the evolution of the HR function.

Personnel people used to go and talk to one employee at a time; difficult conversations used to be part and parcel of their daily routine. Employee relations people used to go and talk to employees in larger groups. HR people don't talk to anyone any more. Many would rather give an employee their P45 than actually have a conversation, because these days HR is all about systems, analysis and data.

In Annabel's view, HR's struggle to earn a seat on the board has caused many HR departments to turn the people button off – firmly and once and for all.

To prove that it contributes to the bottom line, HR has had to become as dispassionate as finance or facilities management. These days, the h for human raises expectations that aren't going to be realized because HR's role can narrow down to protecting the business from the staff.

Another equally important shift has been the offloading of much of HR's traditional transactional stuff, such as annual leave and performance management, away from HR practitioners and onto employee-enabled technology.

A successful HR director nowadays is someone who can select and supervise good systems.

All of this has had a catastrophic effect on HR's role in redundancy. Annabel points out that, although HR staff are well qualified these days, the focus of the CIPD (Chartered Institute of Personnel and Development) syllabus is principally on compliance. Moreover, newer HR practitioners often have absolutely no experience of redundancy.

Annabel's considered opinion is that:

it isn't HR's fault that they're so hopeless with redundancy. Often, they are no more than the manifestation and messenger of the problem. All they do is deliver the message once everything's been decided elsewhere.

She concludes her HR riff on an intriguing note.

We've ended up with the compliance-only model of HR, designed to get employees in, keep them motivated, and then get them out. Non-compliance-related activities don't happen any more. HR spends a lot of time on on-boarding (as recruitment is now called), but what about off-boarding? Maybe it's about time that the 'Sunday Times' started a survey called 'The 100 Best Companies to Leave'?

Moving on to the role that managers play in redundancy, Annabel doesn't pull any punches here either. Her opening salvo is that:

less than 3% of managers in this country have had any formal training in how to be a manager, so is it any wonder that they're not very good at making people redundant? They've got absolutely no basis for doing it.

Although she concedes that managers aren't consciously malevolent, Annabel inclines to the view that they can be both crass and lazy. They also suffer from that very British trait of not wanting to upset anyone.

Managers conflate upsetting people with upsetting themselves because it's very difficult for them to lay off their own team members. This cross-identity factor is acute.

Managers not being able to handle their own emotions is one thing, but there's also evidence that, on occasion, they're prepared to use redundancy for their own ends. Annabel's received plenty of calls for professional help that fall into what she calls 'the scoop-up school of redundancy'. They go something like this:

I've already got a list. There are two groups: the people who really need to go and the others. The others comprise Robert – I've always hated him, and Donna, Graham and Kevin who are a complete pain. Can you find us a method that fits and then just rubber stamp our decision?

This is in direct contravention of Annabel's second golden rule of establishing the method and then implementing it fairly and objectively. Moreover, the scoop-up school can trigger unfair dismissal claims not just from the four employees in the *others* category, but from all the employees in the other group as well.

Annabel recognizes that managers sometimes genuinely believe that they're making fair, sensible and objective decisions, but still end up making random ones. In her view, part of the reason for this is the complete and utter absence of a fit-for-purpose performance management system. In light of that absence, all sorts of approaches flourish.

Two of my particular favourites are the reverse discrimination two-step and the face fit test. Under the first one, managers don't even consider for redundancy those who are gay, pregnant, disabled or belong to an ethnic minority. And they don't seem to realize that they are unlawfully discriminating against the heterosexual able-bodied white male, as well as deliberately not ending up with the strongest team after the cutbacks.

The second one (face fit) crucially depends on how much time people spend down the pub with the rest of the team. This is guaranteed to work against home and part-time workers who are predominantly women, people who work off-site who are discriminated against by distance, and women with school-age children who have to get home to their kids.

Annabel is also increasingly noticing a lack of planning.

Years ago, people used to plan redundancies properly. Now, they phone up and say, 'Can you help? I'm half-way through a redundancy programme and I'm just wondering if...' They don't know what they don't know.

As we near the end of the interview, Annabel returns to a word that she's used repeatedly throughout: 'conversation'.

In redundancy interviews, employees are being subjected to this compliance process which requires the company to be in the right. The HR professional and the manager are so focused on compliance and not making any mistakes that they stop conversations from happening. Avoidance of the conversation becomes the golden rule.

Being of an optimistic cast of mind, I'd like to end on a note of that ilk. Annabel concentrates long and hard.

Some HR directors are trying to change the current model, but changing HR won't really achieve anything for as long as there's cognitive dissonance in the big picture. What this is all about is making HR people and managers understand how to make people redundant and leave them smiling. There may be a useful comparison here between redundancy and death in service when organizations do seem capable of acting with compassion and respect, rather than following the compliance-only model.

Just when I think we're on an upward spiral, Annabel gives me an example of the scale of the prevailing cognitive dissonance.

One of my clients insisted on sending a survey to the employees it had made redundant to glean feedback about the process. I counselled against it, but they did it anyway. To make matters worse, it was a free survey . The client was genuinely surprised at the hostile reaction – and at the arson threat.

Sensing my disappointment at the downward turn, Annabel digs more deeply.

I'd like to see some information about redundancy that's not just statistical. Anecdotal stuff has value. Perhaps your book will help.

Amen to that.

Annabel Kaye is a director of Irenicon Ltd (www.irenicon.co.uk) a specialist employment law and HR consultancy she co-founded in 1980. Anyone at risk of redundancy can download free information from her KoffeeKlatch site (www.koffeeklatch.co.uk). She can also offer employers support in designing, communicating or implementing a redundancy.

Chapter XVIII

Is there a different model of redundancy already out there? The charitable sector: take one.

Dorothy Newton is now retired although, as one of her friends so perceptively remarks, 'she's the busiest retired person I know'. Her final permanent job was as regional director of a charity that supported people who were bringing about change in their community. In that role, she had plenty of experience of redundancy – on both the giving and the receiving end. She shares her thoughts with me.

Dorothy begins by explaining that there's a lot of what she terms 'redundancy light' in the charitable sector because money is always very hand to mouth.

Even though many staff have fixed term contracts and they're always subject to funding, people can still have unrealistic expectations about how long the job's going to last, particularly if things are going well.

These types of redundancies might have been a commonplace occurrence, but Dorothy's approach to them was far from being in the same category.

For me, redundancy isn't an isolated incident, it's part and parcel of the whole employment experience. I made a point of going through all the stages of the formal process. It was important to me both that

193

I was being clear and that what I was saying was clear to the other person. There wasn't a problem in a technical sense because if there's no money, then there's no money. It makes it difficult to fail, but I still wanted to do it properly.

Dorothy acknowledges that almost all of the people who left the charity at the end of a fixed term contract went on to find other fulfilling jobs.

They were an extremely talented group of people, so I'm glad that their talent was obvious to other employers.

Dorothy's next experience of redundancy was of the middleweight variety. It was at a time when a group of employees had to leave the charity because several projects were coming to an end, and a fairly major restructuring was also under way.

The charity didn't have an HR department, so Dorothy decided to hire a freelance HR consultant to help her deal with the situation. She didn't want the consultant to wield the axe on her behalf, but to teach her how to wield it responsibly and respectfully herself. The consultant asked Dorothy what she wanted out of the process, and Dorothy knew immediately.

I want to make it as personal as I can because I want to leave people with their dignity intact.

Dorothy and the consultant worked together until Dorothy knew that:

- she was competent to do it;

- she had to do it; and

- she had to do it right.

I still feel really grateful to that consultant. She supported me and trained me so well that I took all that learning with me into the next phase and was able to use the same model with a different HR professional.

Roll on a couple of years and 'redundancy heavy' comes into play. The charity merged with a social enterprise or, as Dorothy rather ruefully reflects, it didn't:

I know now that there's no such thing as a merger; it was a takeover.

Although Dorothy couldn't see the synergy behind the merger and soon learned that there was a whole cultural mismatch between the two organizations, she respected the CEO's vision and tried to make things work.

Until, that is, the point at which she was no longer allowed to raise funds for her region; that signalled the end of her operation. Dorothy's thoughts focused on her staff:

I wanted to be honest with them, but I didn't want to undermine their trust in the organization. I was trying to be discreet at a time when my staff were hearing rumours from the other regional teams. I ended up feeling like a Victorian parent deciding what was good or bad for the children.

In the end, a series of meetings throughout the organization solved Dorothy's dilemma for her.

Everyone knew the lifetime of their own job, so they could draw their own conclusions.

Even once the knowledge was out in the open, it was still a very difficult situation because some of the programmes that the charity ran were coming to an end imminently while others still had ten years to go. Within the space of a year, Dorothy had to make a dozen people redundant, find suitable successor organizations for the continuing programmes, continue to run the regional office as a going concern, and deal with staff concerns.

One of the most difficult things was that people in the community with whom we were working were upset on our behalf. We had to try and reassure them that they could and would achieve their goals without us. And we had to do that in spite of our own level of anxiety.

Dorothy readily admits that, at times, the situation had a tragicomic feel to it.

We rented our office space from another organization, so I had to keep them informed as we shrank in size. Their FD had one of our organization charts and he developed the habit of crossing out people's faces as they left.

In the midst of all this muddle, Dorothy made up her own mind about how she was going to tackle the redundancies. Although the charity had no central HR function whatsoever, the social enterprise did. However, instead of shuffling the dreaded deed off onto HR, Dorothy followed her instincts: she assumed personal responsibility.

I knew that HR would do it by the book in the sense of doing the absolute minimum, of just covering off all the technicalities, but everyone knows that redundancy is about so much more than that.

When it came to the redundancy meetings with individual staff members, Dorothy and an HR person from the social enterprise conducted them together, but with Dorothy taking the lead. She asked the HR practitioner not to intervene unless she saw and heard Dorothy going wrong – in which case, a swift kick under the table would suffice.

I wanted somebody on my side because I hoped that the staff members would have somebody on theirs. We were very lucky to have an exemplary trade union rep who was prepared to accompany as many people as asked him. He wasn't at all hostile to me, even though I was management. He accompanied me to my individual meeting as well. I'm so glad that I paid my union subs.

Dorothy kept her focus on her team, making sure that they had enough time out of the office to find other jobs. However, she also insisted that a regular office routine be maintained, records be archived and transferred properly, and surplus equipment and supplies be given away thoughtfully. The small group of team members who stayed to the bitter end supported each other during this difficult time and then all moved on into suitable new roles elsewhere.

Dorothy knows that all of her staff now have good jobs and she takes comfort in the hope that none of them was damaged by the way in which they left the charity.

I ask Dorothy what she's learned as a result of having experienced redundancy from both sides of the table.

When you're making people redundant, it's a very lonely place. You have to put your own stuff to one side. You have to simply steel yourself to do it. I didn't feel that I was being horrible. I didn't enjoy making my staff redundant, but I hoped I was doing it as well as I could. I feel very lucky that I had good people who were prepared to stay until the end. Perhaps the fact that everyone knew I was losing my job as well made it easier for all of us.

I was lucky too in that I had two very good role models: a former colleague and my daughter Lucy, both of whom had been made redundant twice. That gave me the confidence that people could come out of it the other side OK.

And as the recipient?

I'm fortunate that it happened at the end of my career, although I still don't understand why HR didn't just wait a couple of months until I was 65, and then I'd have been a non-issue. Also, for me, it would have been a mark of respect if my line manager, the CEO, had come to my redundancy meeting, but he was oblivious to all that. As he took pride in not being a professional manager, I can't say I was surprised.

After having been so heavily involved in redundancy for a year, Dorothy didn't stay in redundant mode for very long. Four days after closing the regional office, she started working as a freelance consultant to a university research programme. This came about thanks to her colleagues in Bristol, whose response to redundancy had been to set up a community interest company (CIC).

Working through the new CIC made life very simple for Dorothy. She didn't have to register as self-employed and deal with complicated tax matters. This swift reassignment:

took the sting out of it for me. I didn't have time to dwell on it.

That proved to be her last paid work, although Dorothy's not really retired in the conventional sense of the word. She's now the chair of another charity and a volunteer for various good causes within her local community.

I'm still using the experience of having to get things right and be objective. There are wider lessons to be learnt than just how to cope with the physical act of making people redundant. For me, the most important thing to pass on is that we need to treat people kindly when they're under threat.

Dorothy Newton is the chair of trustees at Richard Cloudesley's Charity.

Chapter XIX

Is there a different model of redundancy already out there? The charitable sector: take two.

Murielle Maupoint now runs Live It Publishing, publishers of this book; in an earlier incarnation, she spent eight years as the chief executive of a charity that helped homeless young people back into the mainstream of life, education, training, employment and housing.

As we already know from Dorothy's story in the previous chapter, the charitable sector is inherently unstable because funding comes from so many different sources. The financial year end of Murielle's charity was April; every July, she had to tell her staff that the funding still hadn't arrived, so she might not be able to pay them next month. They should feel free to take time off and look for other jobs, and she would support them fully.

I told them that I believed the money would arrive, but I didn't expect them to share that belief. No-one ever left; the staff adopted a 'we'll sink with the ship' attitude.

This was all the more remarkable given that Murielle had a somewhat counter-cultural recruitment policy.

I went out of my way to employ people who didn't have much experience in social care because I wanted to give them a start. I was also keen to have a team comprised of very different personalities so that clients would always find someone to gravitate towards. This had upsides and downsides.

Murielle found herself juggling with the same fixed term contracts issue as Dorothy, although she always tried to find her staff alternative positions within the organization when their original contract came to an end.

Moving from being a project worker to an employment support worker, for example, gives people different skills and experiences. My staff and I had a reciprocal commitment to one another. I wanted to make it work at all costs. Sadly, sometimes, it didn't.

On those occasions, Murielle was very clear about the outcome she wanted: staff members knowing that this was the last resort, that the charity was as upset about it as they were, that they were leaving with their head held high, and were going on to a new opportunity elsewhere.

In my view, redundancy isn't a process; it's about treating people with compassion and respect, and making sure they leave with their self-esteem intact.

Murielle adopted this model even when she had to ask staff to leave because of what she can only describe as 'outrageous behaviour': uploading photos of a naked boyfriend onto an office computer; inviting vulnerable clients back home for a cup of tea; entertaining at the hostel a boyfriend who was on day release from prison; smoking cannabis with clients at Center Parcs.

Not that this kind of behaviour automatically entailed dismissal; it depended on the severity of the misconduct and the impact on clients.

If staff members were prepared to admit that they'd been human and simply made a mistake, then the charity would work to find a way to enable them to stay. The one-time dope smoker now heads up a major arm of the charity.

Even when Murielle was dealing with the girl with the unfortunate taste in boyfriends and photography, who absolutely refused to admit that she was at fault, she still wanted to manage her exit in the way that would be most beneficial and supportive to her.

Murielle advised her to resign, making her aware that the disciplinary procedure could only have one possible outcome, and that it would be better for her not to have an instance of dismissal on her employment record. The girl saw the wisdom of this and complied, but Murielle still felt as though she'd let her down.

Murielle realized early on that the social care field attracts people who've had similar life experiences to those affecting the clients.

The mentality seems to be 'I've been homeless and I know what that's like, so I want to help the homeless'. Of course, this doesn't necessarily mean that they're going to be any good at it. To be successful, they need to have done a lot of self-help and personal development stuff first.

To make this come true, Murielle trained every single staff member in NLP in the belief that this would give everyone a common language, a shared set of assumptions, an understanding of the whys and wherefores behind behaviour. It seemed to pay dividends; it also strongly supported Murielle's view of work.

I believe in having a close relationship with employees. Work's a huge part of our life: it should be enriching and supportive, giving people the opportunity to grow, develop, learn and have fun.

In parallel with Dorothy's story in the previous chapter, Murielle's charity also merged with another organization although, in this case, they both had a very similar ethos in terms of how they worked with their staff. I ask Murielle how she handled the merger.

Transparency was essential. We were very good at letting people know what was going on at every stage. We asked for staff input and arranged reciprocal visits. We were very clear about which head office jobs would be at risk, told the four employees concerned, and offered to support them in their efforts to find a new position. They all said: 'We don't want to work anywhere else. We'll take the consequences, whatever they are.' I felt humbled by their loyalty.

Murielle believes that the key to managing redundancies effectively is keeping staff informed:

If you don't know something, say so; but do tell people what you're doing, how you're doing it, what the worst case scenario would be, and what you're putting in place to manage that.

Does Murielle think that this model could work in large organizations? In her view, the pre-requisites are trust, honesty, flexibility, and good communications. She thinks corporates suffer from at least two disadvantages:

- they don't have the same kind of flexibility as smaller organizations;

and

- they have systems and processes, rules and procedures that have often been written by those who have no people skills whatsoever.

Large organizations get stuck in the process. However, I do think there's a middle ground between what I did and what corporates currently do, although there'd need to be a willingness to move towards it as well as a culture to support it. As long as the starting point for redundancy is fear of being sued, it will continue to be an isolating experience for everyone involved.

Although Murielle concedes that redundancies are often a consequence of the economic climate, she still doesn't believe that they should ever come as a surprise to employees. If they do, in her opinion, management hasn't fulfilled its moral obligations to the workforce.

If you manage performance well and respond appropriately, then dismissals should be a rarity. There should be an on-going discussion in which redundancy is one possible option. As the future plays out, the options narrow.

Murielle also takes the view that organizations often under-rate their employees in redundancy situations, by not taking into account how flexible they can be, how willing they are to get by on less money, to do without perks, how much they appreciate being involved and asked for their opinion.

This approach lessens the pain; it also enables employees to operate at a higher level because they can focus on their work without worrying about the future.

In an eerie echo of Dorothy's words, Murielle concludes:

People can hide behind HR, but for me redundancy is a very personal thing. I felt huge pride and satisfaction when employees left us with a smile on their face. I felt as though I had done my job. There would be fewer problems and less waste of money if organizations didn't mishandle redundancy so spectacularly. In my book, redundancy is part of the everyday employment experience.

Murielle Maupoint is the author of 'The Essential NLP Practitioner's Handbook' and founder of Live It Ventures (www.liveit.com and www.liveitpublishing.com).

Part IV

Redundancy Stories

Chapter XX

Aleksandr

As his name suggests, Aleksandr is Russian. He's also a high-flying, high-earning marketing professional making his way swiftly up the corporate ladder in a global advertising agency. He's not expecting to be made redundant, but he is.

After almost eight years, during three of which he had led the team and developed an unrivalled knowledge of the client, brand and territory for which he was responsible, Aleksandr thought he had gone beyond the redundancy threshold. The events of 11 May 2011 proved him wrong.

His brief redundancy meeting left him with a cocktail of negative feelings – shock, anger, unfairness – as well as a profound sense of detachment from the people, the projects, the problems; even the profession and the industry. He left the office for a cigarette and a coffee, and didn't return until he was called back to discuss details.

It takes a couple of weeks to get used to the idea that it's happened and that there's no way back. What saved me was the memory of what I am and where I came from – years before I had the job. Happiness is about yourself rather than about a job or money; the wind still blows and the sun still shines. You have to let the job go and create some solid space in your head before you can move on.

Aleksandr was so angry about the way his redundancy had been conducted that he decided to seek legal advice. His anger and disappointment continued throughout the two months it took to reach a settlement. When the final letter arrived though, he felt a huge sense of relief.

After the dust had settled, Aleksandr considered three options:

- asking the client for whom he had worked during his time at the agency for a job;

- finding another job in the same industry; and

- doing something different which he would enjoy.

He dismissed the first one because the client hadn't supported him during his redundancy, and the second one because his sense of detachment was so strong that he believed in his heart of hearts that his days in that industry were at an end. That left him with option three.

By his own admission, Aleksandr is one of those people who never knew what he wanted to do in life. Although, during his career, he learned to pretend that he had a five-year plan, he secretly always agreed with the Russian saying that:

If you want to make God laugh, tell Him about your plans.

Aleksandr was fortunate enough to be able to survive on his savings while he sorted himself out. He developed the habit of distracting himself from his troubles by spending hours in the garden which he'd completely re-designed a couple of years previously. During that process, he'd casually thought that maybe, one day, he could make a living as a garden designer.

He started exploring the possibilities: he enrolled on a learn-at-home landscaping course, bought himself a basic garden design tool kit, agreed to transform a friend's garden. Crucially, he cut himself some slack.

With the loss of my job, I'd lost money, identity, and the freedom that comes from money. But a job is only an acquired identity that helps you to conform with society. Once you reconnect with what you were before, you lose the fear of not having that acquired identity. I found the strength to be OK with not going to work, to give myself the time and the space to focus on what could be possible for me.

At this point in Aleksandr's story, a friend of a friend mentioned a potential job in the industry he'd just left so unceremoniously. All he felt at the prospect was complete aversion. He concentrated on his gardening project, realizing that he was back in the territory of a job being a hobby, the way it had been at the beginning of his marketing career. He bought a web domain name, organized business cards, started developing a business plan.

Aleksandr had never run his own business before so, although he was feeling confident, he was also feeling scared, thinking that he didn't know how to do it. He was stuck, caught in a conflict between his head and his heart. His head wanted him to return to corporate life, in spite of all his misgivings; his heart wanted him to stay in the garden.

Nine months after he was made redundant, two very significant things happened. First, Aleksandr heard that the job that had been mooted in August was now a definite role rather than just a vague outline. Second, he renewed his acquaintance with a woman who had been a client of such long-standing that she'd become a friend.

During a wine-fuelled discussion of his redundancy, she felt able to point out that, although his technical knowledge and expertise were outstanding, his people skills weren't. Suddenly, everything fell into place. He had a new perspective on his career to date, his redundancy, and his plans for the future. He knew what he was going to do.

First, though, he had to rush home and thank his partner for trying to tell him about his people skills much earlier on – at a time when he just wasn't ready for feedback. Aleksandr sailed through two interviews and has now started his new job. Yes, he's back in the industry that he previously thought he'd left for all time.

The initial contract is only for six months but, if Aleksandr proves his worth, he'll have a permanent job. He's pretty determined that he's going to make that happen. So determined in fact that he's hired a coach to help him bring his people skills up to the same superlative level as his technical ones.

Chapter XXI

Cathy

Cathy had spent 20 years as an operations manager in the world of character-licensed bubble bath before redundancy struck for the second time. She spent the last year of her business career reconciling the production systems of her original employer with those of the larger company that had bought it.

Cathy sincerely believed that, once she'd proved that packing and shipping could be done more time- and cost-effectively in the UK than in China, there'd be a future for her and her team. Events proved her wrong: once the systems were reconciled, they were all out of a job.

Once out, Cathy had a epiphany.

I think I've been wasting my life. I'm a useful person and I'm going to go and do something useful by working in the third sector.

Her soon-to-be-ex-employer had provided access to outplacement specialists, so Cathy decided to make the most of them while she was waiting for all the loose ends to be tied. She learned three golden rules:

- number one: treat outplacement as if it's a full-time job – turn up each day and work hard.

- number two: send application letters to named individuals rather than to job-titles.

- number three: if you want to change sectors, treat it as a research project.

Cathy treated rule number one as gospel, got through to interview for a high-powered job courtesy of the second, and ended up on a completely different planet in career terms because of the third.

As a result of making a casual remark about her research project in the office, Cathy found herself talking to the regional director of a charity that helped people bring about change in their community. The director's central office colleague, a heavyweight ex-Civil Service veteran, was also in attendance.

Cathy had received a good pay-out from the bubble bath company and was expecting to take a year out. She already had this recurring thought about business skills being transferable, but all she was doing at this stage was research – as per the outplacement advice. Then the ex-Civil Servant gave her an overview of the charity's difficulties and finished challengingly with:

So what would you do with that lot?

I'd do this, that, and the other.

Why don't you come and do it then?

It wasn't quite that simple: the director had to find the funding from somewhere and also get approval for the new post. Moreover, Cathy had to accept a three-month contract at a much reduced salary. Nevertheless, she found herself working at the charity in remarkably short order. She was still in a sabbatical frame of mind and she regarded three months as an ideal period of time in which to learn something useful.

Non-monetary things are important as well.

By the time she started, Cathy already had a job lined up to go to once the three months came to an end. Not that she ever got there. As far as Cathy was concerned, the charity's problem was blindingly obvious: it operated in an environment that was heavily biased towards admin and paperwork, but the outreach workers didn't necessarily understand just how important this was. Cathy netted it right down for them:

If we don't have all the right pieces of paper in the right place at the right time, we won't get paid – simple as that.

Her first task was to break down all the processes into their individual tasks and then work with the IT person to design a computer system to keep track of everything. Once the computer system was up and running and the admin was beginning to become more streamlined, Cathy turned her attention to the split between the outreach workers and the admin team.

I understood that some of the outreach workers thought it was more important to be out and doing than bothering with paperwork. I went out and got involved with them so that they could see what I was bringing into the charity: a business way of doing things.

Cathy also took over responsibility for compiling the numbers, figures and hours for the numerous government tenders, freeing up the director's time for higher-level, more strategic activities.

I didn't know anything about social outcomes and still don't, but I do know about procedural stuff – filling out forms, keeping receipts, keeping track, getting the paperwork done.

Cathy was so successful that before too long all the other regions of the charity were clamouring for their own operations manager. She became an indispensable member of the team; the three-month contract turned into an 18-month contract, and Cathy only left for a very different reason.

At the age of 44 and after 18 years with the same partner, I fell pregnant. Our son is definitely the baby of that charity. He'd never have happened if I'd stayed in toiletries.

Tough times were ahead. Cathy suffered from post-natal psychosis, and had to spend three months in an institution undergoing electric shock treatment while her partner looked after her son and her friends looked after her partner.

As she gradually regained her health, Cathy realized that she wanted to be a stay-at-home mum so she told the charity that she wouldn't be going back. She'd have liked another baby, but the powerful anti-psychosis drugs helped induce an early menopause. In spite of this, Cathy's overriding emotion is gratitude.

The person who got made redundant seven years ago and the person I am now barely inhabit the same planet. When I got made redundant the first time, I knew I could survive because I found another job the same week. Second time around, everything was right for me to take a massive leap.

Under what other set of circumstances would I ever have changed my life? I'd have been in that job, in that rat race with a really good salary, until I retired. Now I earn a pittance, but I have a portfolio life that I absolutely love. I keep volunteering for things that I don't know how to do.

Cathy works as a clerk to a statutory body mainly from home, is a school governor, helps run a toddler group, and is involved in her local community in ways too various to mention.

She sums up her experience of redundancy thus:

It was good that I got made redundant. When you're working, you get caught up in the daily pressures of your job. When you lose that job, you can step back and ask yourself: 'Why was I doing that?' I went to the charity to find out what I didn't know; it turned out to be a whole lot more than I'd thought.

Chapter XXII

Darcy

Darcy served in the Army for 15 years. When he left, his resettlement package included training as an IT analyst. He easily secured a job in the financial services sector and, for the first two years, everything was great.

Many of his colleagues were also ex-Forces, so the team gelled really well; there was a buzzing and dynamic feel to the workplace; the bonuses and expense accounts were good. In return, Darcy and his colleagues worked hard, putting in between 60 and 80 hours each week.

Then, in year three, a process known as *trimming the fat* began. Those who were close to retirement were helped out the door – with massive pay-outs; the young bucks moved up the ladder to take their place.

Next came the restructuring: teams merged, even when it made no organizational sense. With roles duplicated within the new teams, the redundancies and re-training offers started in earnest.

One morning, Darcy's boss – a senior professional with 12 years' service and seemingly limitless loyalty – asked Darcy to cover his desk as he had to go to a meeting. When Darcy's mobile rang an hour later, he was surprised to hear his boss's voice against the background clatter of coffee cups.

I'm in Caffè Nero across the road. I've been made redundant. Security marched me off the premises and wouldn't let me back to my desk. So can you bring my phone, wallet and briefcase down to me? Also, can you just scoot over to my desk, log in with my password, run this programme and then log out?

Darcy complied, not knowing that his boss's parting gift was a programme that deleted all the IT group's passwords so that no-one could log in. It created such havoc that the company had to hire an external consultant to sort out the mess.

Darcy's first thought was to wonder whether the organization was going to treat him in the same way. Not that he had any particular attachment to his job: he was only doing it for the money. He wanted to earn enough to set himself up as a plumber: the trade he'd abandoned to join the Army.

Things went rapidly downhill. The workforce cuts had been so savage that the workload became impossible. The messages coming down the line became blunt to the point of brutality.

The only way we can keep you on is to do away with your bonuses.

Darcy and his colleagues knew full well that the senior people were still getting large bonuses. They kept their heads down and carried on working, but realized that the fundamental bond of trust between employer and employee was already broken beyond repair. Come appraisal time, Darcy's new manager pushed his bonus notification across the desk, saying:

This reflects all your hard work over the past year. That's how bad it's been.

The bonus figure was zero.

Darcy knew that his boss was pushing him to leave, and that's exactly what many of his colleagues did. Not Darcy: he dug in for the duration.

He was completing his plumbing training and certification at night school; it suited him to stay. Life at work was becoming increasingly unpleasant though; very few friendly faces now remained in his team.

The announcement of more redundancies came in a low profile meeting at the end of the year.

The packages won't be anywhere near as generous as previously and we're leaving it up to the line managers to decide – with advice from HR – who goes next.

Darcy knew for sure that he'd be made redundant at some point, so he started working nine to five Monday to Friday, as per his contract. He'd previously been working three weekends out of four, even though his contract stipulated that weekend working was only required in critical situations where the company's share price would be affected when the Stock Exchange opened on Monday morning. His attitude was now set in concrete.

Darcy went to HR to tell them that he'd like to be made redundant.

You can't volunteer, but we'll make a note that you're not happy.

The consequences of that note became apparent at noon on a Friday some months later. Darcy was off sick at home in Chelmsford when a motorbike courier from London rang the doorbell. He handed Darcy a large envelope; a redundancy offer and letter nestled inside.

You've got to sign it immediately so that I can get it back to the HR department in London before close of business tonight.

I'm sorry mate, but I really need to think about this. I'm not signing.

Courier doesn't budge.

I'm sure you'll get paid for your return journey. I'm not signing it, no matter how long you stand there. I know this is rude, but I'm closing the door on you now.

After a brief mobile call, the courier disappeared.

Darcy phoned his previous boss – the one who'd been marched off the premises. He laughed at the news, but gave Darcy some valuable advice.

Don't go anywhere near any of the employment lawyers recommended by the company. Find yourself someone local.

Darcy did – and that specialist took care of everything, including spotting the fact that Darcy's pension entitlement was linked to his previous pay grade, rather than his current one. He also secured a larger settlement for Darcy and £500 for himself, rather than the £300 offered by Darcy's employer.

Darcy had one final conversation with HR. They offered him redeployment, but Darcy knew with absolute certainty that he would no longer fit in anywhere in that organization. He never went back to the office.

I didn't really do anything for a month. I'd expected to be in IT for five or ten years, so it was a shock. I bought my tools and my van and set up my plumbing business, but it was two months before I could put an ad in the paper. I didn't really want any work because I was so worried that no-one was going to call or even be happy with my work or estimates.

Three months after leaving, Darcy finally received his box of possessions – minus his squash shoes and racket, but he was past caring by then. He was already enjoying the next phase of his life.

I'm glad about the redundancy now because it gave me a push. It came a year too early because I hadn't completed the gas training of my plumbing course. I had to pay for that myself from the redundancy money, so it took a little longer to complete. Even so, it forced me to get out there and work on my own, and it's proving to be a great experience.

Chapter XXIII

Joanna

Joanna works in retail merchandising. She'd been in a new role – new for her and new for the company – for six months when redundancy struck. Colleagues left suddenly and abruptly, but good news followed: there weren't going to be any more redundancies.

Shortly afterwards, Joanna's line manager called her into a meeting room where the head of HR was waiting. The two of them spent so much time going all round the houses, trying to soften the blow, that Joanna had to ask for clarification. In the end, she understood the message: they were making her role redundant, but wanted to keep her within the business. She had 28 days in which to find another job within the company or she would be made redundant. She could take as much time off as she needed to pursue opportunities both within and outside the company, and the company would help her in any way it could.

They also went through the redundancy package with me. Bearing in mind I'd only been there for six months, I thought it was incredibly generous. My emotions were very mixed. I was disappointed because one of my reasons for taking this role was the size of the organization: I'd thought my job would be secure. I was worried about the future, but I also felt relieved because I hadn't been enjoying the job. Perhaps this was a way out.

Joanna didn't hear any more for two days and was beginning to feel decidedly twitchy. At this point, her line manager took her to one side:

I'd like to tell your team of 15 what's going on, but I won't unless you are happy for me to do so.

Joanna felt torn: she'd wanted to keep the news to herself and just deal with it on her own, but also realized that her team did need to know, particularly since it had already suffered during the earlier round of redundancies. Her manager handled it so well that, in spite of the initial shock and disappointment, everyone felt reassured. Even Joanna benefited: now the news was out in the open, she would no longer have to make excuses for her job-hunting absences.

The next day, HR contacted Joanna. At the subsequent meeting, the HR manager was positive and encouraging, making Joanna aware of all sorts of opportunities, both internally and externally, and putting her in touch with sources of professional support.

I came out of that meeting with a completely open mind: a new role here, a move to another retailer, volunteering for a charity, retraining as an accountant? After all, I didn't have any commitments that would force me to take any job going.

Joanna's employer had arranged for an outplacement agency to have an on-site office so that it could help those who were leaving. Even though Joanna wasn't in that category yet, she was still able to make use of the service to help her update her CV. She also went to see a recruitment consultant who was a personal contact of the HR manager. Joanna's line manager was more than happy for her to take as much time out of the office as she needed.

Halfway though her 28 day consultation period, Joanna was scouring the company intranet for potential new roles and HR was doing the same on her behalf. One interesting opportunity fell by the wayside because Joanna didn't have enough buying experience, and volunteering and accountancy also proved to be dead ends at this point in her life.

I had days of feeling really low about everything. I kept thinking that I've only got two weeks left and then I'll be redundant.

It was at this point that a job as a project manager within a completely different department popped up. HR arranged the interview and the maths test: a source of some annoyance to Joanna given that she'd been working in merchandising since the year dot. The news that her score was the highest ever achieved mollified her somewhat; the news that the job was hers if she wanted it mollified her completely.

With only a week to go, the merchandising director called Joanna and asked her if she'd like to move into core merchandising, even though all her previous roles had been in branch merchandising.

I'd always thought that I was too senior to make the switch, but the director assured me that it would be OK, that the company would protect my salary for 12 months on the assumption that by this time I'd have worked my way up to where I needed to be.

I now had two offers in my final week. Both were great opportunities and I didn't have a clue what to do. It was a real head versus heart conflict.

Joanna decided to go back to the outplacement specialists for some advice; at the end of the one-hour session, she had her answer. That session made Joanna realize that what was most important to her at this stage of her life was security.

I didn't know how long the project management job would last and what roles I would be able to move on to afterwards, but if you can do core merchandising you'll never be unemployed because you can always get a job somewhere else.

With time in full countdown mode, Joanna was still worried. She was, after all, moving into a completely new role. What would happen if she either didn't like it or wasn't any good at it? HR reassured her that everything would be reviewed after three months. If either party wasn't happy, Joanna would still be eligible for her original redundancy package. She realized immediately that she had nothing to lose.

I started the new job and it was far from ideal. I don't think the company had quite thought it all through as the change had happened so quickly. They placed me in a team where I was shadowing a colleague but had no set roles or responsibilities of my own. I had to start at the bottom because I didn't know anything, but working and learning on the job was really difficult.

The one thing that made Joanna's life slightly easier was the support she received from HR. The HR manager was still positive and proactive, making sure that Joanna was given every assistance – from her colleagues, her superiors, and the training department – to make the new arrangement work.

After three months, Joanna still wasn't convinced that she was making enough progress in her new role. When she voiced her concerns, the company extended her eligibility for redundancy to nine months. Although this made her feel better, the breakthrough she needed didn't come until her transfer to a different department – and to a lower level within a team.

With a specific role and my own responsibilities, I started to really learn the job. I was finally where I needed to be.

Even after six months on this accelerated learning path, Joanna knew that she wasn't going to make the grade by the 12-month deadline. She simply wouldn't be operating at a level that would justify her protected salary.

Once again, she spoke to HR. The upshot was an agreed lower cap on her salary and a stepped quarterly decrease down to that cap. As it turned out, the company never did cut Joanna's salary. After two years in core merchandising, Joanna returned to the managerial rung she'd been on in her original job, even skipping over one grade completely. Four years after her threatened redundancy, she's still doing – and loving – the same job.

Reflecting on her near-redundancy experience, Joanna believes the most important lesson she learned was the importance of being open-minded and staying as positive as possible.

That was some of the feedback I got from HR: the reason they helped me so much and so often was because I stayed positive and professional throughout. I think you need to try and appreciate redundancy as a new opportunity. Take a look at everything, especially if you've been in a career for ten or 15 years. Even think about taking some time off or doing something completely different.

Chapter XXIV

Marie

Marie is an American digital marketing professional; she's proud of her profession and her professionalism, but she no longer plies her trade on behalf of the corporate world. She tells me why.

Marie's story begins when she was working for a small American company based in New York. The company decided to open an office in the UK; Marie agreed to take charge. After nine months of punishingly hard work during which she worked 12 hours a day and did everything that needed to be done to get the UK operation up and running, Marie heard some devastating news.

In spite of the fact that the London office was doing really good business, the parent company decided that it could no longer afford to keep it open. All six employees, including Marie, were to be made redundant. Everyone whom Marie had recruited had an employment contract; she didn't. Her employers took advantage of this loophole: everyone – apart from Marie – would receive four weeks' pay in lieu of notice; Marie would receive nothing.

Nothing daunted, Marie shipped up at her local Citizens' Advice Bureau for some free advice. The legal expert penned a letter to Marie's American employer on her behalf: by default, in Marie's case, they would have to honour the employment conditions included in all the other contracts. If the case ended up in court, they would undoubtedly have to pay the four weeks' salary in lieu of notice.

While this was all going on in the background, Marie did her level best to make the redundancy as painless as possible for her fellow employees.

I hired all those people and they felt like friends, so I was really upset at having to make them redundant. For me, it was a very personal responsibility. I made a point of telling them whatever I knew just as soon as I had more news.

Eventually, Marie's employer paid her the same as everyone else, but by then the damage was done.

It was a completely distressing experience. I'd pulled out all the stops for that company. Even so, when it came to the crunch, they didn't flinch from just flicking me aside. It's directed my beliefs and behaviour ever since. I vowed that whatever work I did, I was going to get appropriate payment for it.

Between losing that job and finding her next one – with a large internet service provider, Marie found out that she was pregnant. In what threatened to be a repeating pattern, unexpected news intervened again. Within three months of joining, Marie learned that the company was up for sale. This was welcome – and very heady – news. In the middle of the dotcom boom, the company was worth millions. Everyone was in line for a potential windfall; individual statements put flesh on the figures.

Then, in March 2001, the dotcom bubble burst. The company's value dropped dramatically; the statements were irrelevant: no-one was going to get anything. The company sold for a knock-down price. Management was adamant that there would be no voluntary redundancies.

As Marie had yet to complete her probationary period, she knew that her only entitlement would be statutory maternity pay. With nothing to lose, she took her destiny into her own hands. Marie asked her boss to make her redundant, even though voluntary redundancy wasn't an option.

Not only did her boss agree to redundancy with three months' pay, he deliberately waited until the day after Marie's probationary period expired before he did the deed, so Marie also received an additional three months' pay in lieu of notice.

I still regard that man as a saint. He was absolutely key: he treated me like a human being at a time when he could have been forgiven for focusing on the loss of his own seriously large potential windfall. It's not as if we had a personal relationship; we'd go out for a few drinks, but that was all. He treated me with respect and that's why it was such a different experience from the first time.

Marie returned the respect. During her exit interview, an independent legal adviser provided by the union suggested that she could push for more money, hinting that she might have been discriminated against because of her pregnancy.

I felt as if I had enough. I'd only been there six months and I walked away with six months' pay which was very generous. The fact that one guy just did the right thing completely changed my life. If he hadn't done that, I would have been wounded because of losing two jobs in a row.

Marie was able to take a year off for maternity leave without having to worry about money, and then spent two years freelancing. When one of her clients offered her a full-time job, she took it, but only for a couple of years: until she fell pregnant for the second time. She resumed her freelance lifestyle in 2005 and has been self-employed ever since.

Being a freelancer is a dream: I get paid for the hours I put in and I get treated with respect and appreciation. I have to put in the hours and deliver the work, but I was doing that anyway.

I ask Marie what she's learned from her double dip into redundancy. She goes into passionate mode.

I work the way I do now because of how I was treated. Now that I'm at the stage in life when I can be fully freelance, I'm not going to give any employer the opportunity to screw me over. I'll have a professional working relationship with corporates, but I'm not going to have an emotional and loyal relationship with them. I reserve my loyalty for my clients. It would take an awful lot for an employer to convince me to go and work full-time and, even then, I'd have to feel masses of respect before I'd be willing to do that.

Does she have any words of wisdom for those of us who are going through it now?

Necessity is the mother of invention. Being made redundant is an opportunity to realize who you are and what you can do and what your ambitions are. Sometimes, it can be the kick up the arse we need in order to do what we really want to do.

Chapter XXV

Naomi

Naomi Lowde is the second person in this book I met through Twitter. She's someone who's responded to the blight of redundancy in an absolutely extraordinary way: by writing, producing and appearing in (needs must) a musical on the topic.

Naomi may now be known as the creator of 'Redundancy The Musical', but in 2010 she was working in social care policy in the public sector.

In the autumn of that year, she found herself in the middle of a redundancy programme whose aim was to halve the workforce. As the workplace deteriorated and people became disempowered, Naomi decided to write a musical. Her epiphany came during a redundancy-related group meeting when she drifted off and imagined her colleagues singing and dancing their frustrations away.

When she told her colleagues about the musical, some of them thought she was joking and laughed at the concept. They were completely unaware that Naomi was very serious about her vision. In turn, Naomi interpreted the laughter as a sign of encouragement; she knew that she was onto a good idea.

By October of that year, she knew that she wanted to write the musical more than she wanted a social care job. However, Naomi went through the redundancy process, partly out of curiosity; she even sat through an interview for one of the jobs. A couple of days before Christmas, news of her redundancy came through.

Naomi was so in the zone: living her dream, fulfilling her passion – call it what you will – that she didn't let the impending redundancy prevent her from starting work on the musical while she still had her day job. She began composing the music in October 2010; the words flew onto the screen from January and March 2011, when she rushed home from work at night and during the weekends. The first draft was complete.

Emma Baxter, a colleague of Naomi's sister, agreed to read the second draft. Describing it as 'an exciting script', she readily agreed to direct the musical. The summer passed in a whirl of auditions, growing the social media, recording and uploading demos of the songs. That's without mentioning the website and the search for sponsors and venues.

The story had its bumpy moments, its unexpected twists and turns. But what's so amazing about Naomi is that she wasn't fazed by any of it. At one point, I enquire whether she had any relevant experience.

Not really. The fact that I didn't know how to put on a musical somehow wasn't an issue. I've always been around music and in various indie bands. Plus, I've always loved to write. I've written numerous short stories, poems, lyrics and a novel. But when my laptop was stolen a few years ago – with all my non-backed up writings, I accepted it as a sign that writing and I weren't destined to be...until the flame rekindled years later.

By the time 'Redundancy The Musical' hit the stage at the Hen and Chickens Theatre in Highbury and Islington in February 2012, Naomi had spent almost a year living and breathing it, working up to 70 hours a week, and working with Emma to manage the expectations of cast and crew. She also had to manage her long-suffering and supportive husband Steve.

I can't help myself. I have to ask her 'why?' Her response is disarmingly simple.

This was something that I had to do, something that I knew I would always regret if I didn't do. During the redundancy process, people get treated as an item to be ticked off the agenda, usually urgently. After it's over, they just become another statistic. I wanted them to know that this musical was for them.

By Naomi's own admission, 'Redundancy The Musical' wasn't your average musical: it featured indie band music and lyrics that didn't always rhyme. Given that Naomi's not your average musical producer, this probably shouldn't have come as a surprise. I ask her what's she's learned.

I've just learned so much. In terms of redundancy, I know that people go though a spectrum of emotions but, in the end, most of them are incredibly resilient and resourceful. They think of ways to adapt to a forced change.

In terms of the musical, I learnt a lot of new skills, had an amazing adventure with new people, enjoyed a lot of hardworking fun, ended up achieving more than I'd expected and moving way beyond my past comfort zones.

One of the most important things I learned was that there's immense joy in acting with conviction – regardless of how things turn out and no matter how ridiculous they seem. Working on something you believe in is empowering; it feels like living and growing...rather than existing.

Naomi always knew that her musical venture wasn't about money, but her marital finances suffered to the point where she and husband Steve could no longer afford to live in their present situation. So, a week before the musical's debut, Steve successfully applied for a job in Hong Kong – a place that had always had a certain attraction for both of them.

Instead of taking the musical to the next level immediately after its debut as Naomi had originally planned, she spent two months preparing for her international move. I ask her to reflect on her experience.

After I'd been made redundant and while I was working on the musical, I applied for 25+ jobs and didn't get a single interview. That was depressing, but it helped focus my energies on the show. My redundancy forced me to walk another path. One year and 26 days after being made redundant, I shipped up in Hong Kong, after having written and produced a musical. It's all felt like a whirlwind of reshaping.

I know that the whole experience will shape my future. I have hope and scope for a future that involves writing scripts for both stage and film. And who knows what else the future holds? Maybe another run of 'Redundancy the Musical' at some stage?

Chapter XXVI

Paul

Paul's worked in the automotive industry ever since his dad got him his first job in the body shop of a local garage at the age of 14. He left it unwillingly and regretfully after the accident and repair centre that had been a huge part of his life for 24 years passed into new ownership three years ago. Paul tells me how redundancy went for him.

As is so often the case, it all started swimmingly. When the potential new owners were doing their due diligence – going through the accounts, making sure all the numbers added up – they cosied up to Paul big time, telling him that they wanted him on their side. They reassured that there'd still be a place for him within the centre because they wanted to keep themselves out of the day-to-day operations and concentrate on building up the business.

Even after the sale went through, things were OK for the first couple of months. Then it turned nasty.

Initially, they needed my nous. Of course they did. I'd run the place for 24 years and I was the one who did the books.

It was because of his familiarity with the financials that Paul realized that, with the two new owners on board as directors, the staff overheads were going to be unsustainable. Without ever making anything explicit, the owners decided that Paul's colleague who would be retiring in a couple of years could stay. Paul would have to go.

Their strategy consisted of making life as difficult as possible for me, backing me into a corner, and then being spiteful and nasty. They did everything they could to prevent me from doing my job properly. When they took over, I was general manager and I reported directly to the board. First, they moved me from general manager to office manager, then from office manager to workshop manager. That was bad enough, but then one of their wives came and took over the accounts department and she badmouthed me at every opportunity.

In spite of the stress, the sabotage and the knowledge that the owners wanted him to give up and walk away from the job he loved, Paul just kept working. And carried on doing so for a whole year. Then he went away for a week's holiday; when he got back, the owners told him that they wanted to make him redundant.

They finally got it: piling on the pressure wasn't going to make me leave.

They said that they couldn't see a position for Paul in the company in the future, and asked him if he could. He was feeling so stressed and down by this point that he simply agreed with them. He knew that, even if he'd said 'yes', there was absolutely no possibility of things working out long-term.

At that stage, it became a question of how I'd leave the company rather than if.

As Paul now had nothing to lose, he decided to sue his employers for constructive dismissal. In the end, the case didn't go anywhere but it did provide Paul with another three months' salary while it was under consideration. It also had another unintended consequence which Paul discovered later. His employers had found someone to replace him but, because the redundancy and dismissal procedure took such a long time, they had to let that person go.

Those three months were almost unbearable. My employers didn't speak to me. It was really uncomfortable, not just for me but for everyone else as well. They all knew what was going on, but I had to pretend that I didn't know that they knew and vice versa.

Paul's employers kept playing games until the bitter end by not telling him when his last working day would be. He turned up as usual one morning and received a cheque and a curt command that he could keep his company car until his employers wanted it back.

I took the car back when requested and that was that: 24 years of my life over and done with. There was no closure, no goodbye, no celebration. It was a year before I could bring myself to talk to anyone there. I felt unworthy, disappointed, a failure. When a friend rang my work number shortly after I'd left, she was told that she'd dialled a wrong number, that I'd never worked there. That was what it felt like, as though I'd never existed in that company.

Paul stayed in that state for pretty much the whole of the next year, until he sought some professional help from a coach. He regards this as a turning point because getting all his feelings of unworthiness and failure out of his head and into the open changed his relationship to them, and enabled him to see them from a different perspective.

I ask Paul what else helped and he mentions his income protection insurance policy, although he is far more equivocal about this. With hindsight, he regards it as both a curse and a blessing.

It was good in that it took care of me financially, but bad in that it stopped me from pushing myself forward into something new.

Three years on, Paul still doesn't have a full-time job. He's worked intermittently, sometimes in the automotive industry and sometimes with friends, but he's remarkably upbeat. I ask him to reflect on what he's learned from his redundancy experience.

For me, it's all about balance. For 30 years, I worked 55 hours a week plus every other Saturday, and I thought that was the lifestyle I wanted. Now that I've experienced the polar opposite, I realize that I was missing out on lots of other things. Over the past three years, I've taken time out for myself – with my partner, family, friends and house.

Paul tells me, with irony in his voice, that balance has become such a big issue for him that he's just talked himself out of his latest job: helping a friend to develop his landscape gardening business. He realized that his friend was working so hard and so long each week that he didn't have any spare time to enjoy the fruits of his labours. He spoke up; his friend recognized the wisdom of his words; scaled back his operations; Paul is at a loose end again.

I ask him if he has any regrets.

Not really; being a good friend is a priority. Plus, I feel as though I've been through the whole cycle now: stressful job, no job, non-taxing job – and that was important.

I'm proud of the fact that I've managed to keep myself afloat for the past three years, but now I want something different.

What would something different look and feel like for Paul?

My dad died when he was 70; if I've only got 20 years left, then I want to enjoy them. Whatever I do next, I want to enjoy it, I want it to be the reason I get up in the morning, the reason why I'm part of something bigger than myself, the reason my life has structure and meaning. I know that there's a bigger world out there, that the world opens up – sometimes in big ways, sometimes in small ones. The key is finding out what you want to do. Once you know that, you can do anything you want.

Chapter XXVII

Rebecca

Rebecca now works as a coach and a counsellor; she's had two experiences of redundancy. First time around, her job went; second time around, her job remained.

Rebecca was in her early thirties and working as a graphic designer in an advertising agency when she decided to go travelling for a year. The agency not only kept her job open for her; when she returned, they promoted her to studio manager. This suited Rebecca down to the ground because she'd already developed an interest in counselling. As she now worked from 1 pm to 8 pm, she could also embark on her counselling course.

It was soon after this that the first phase of redundancies occurred. All the staff noticed the ironic coincidence of the directors driving up in new, expensive cars on the same day as they announced the first job cuts. Rebecca counted herself lucky not to be one of the first to go, but was under no illusions: she knew her time would come. She prepared herself by noticing what was happening, thinking about how she would react and researching what her rights and entitlements were.

The agency's policy was that those who had been made redundant had to leave the office on the same day as they heard the news. Rebecca noticed that the people who left in an angry, bitter and resentful frame of mind, without even saying goodbye, were those who found it hardest to find alternative work. She decided that she was going to leave the organization on a hopeful and positive note.

When she received a phone call from the finance director, she knew that the axe was about to fall. Even though she had to confront five directors in the boardroom, Rebecca knew precisely what she wanted: a long lunch, a long goodbye, and the opportunity to make the most of her last day at work. And that's precisely what she did, in spite of the suspicious looks that this behaviour evoked from the directors.

Rebecca managed to hold herself together until she got on the Tube; that was when the floodgates opened and she cried all the way home. A few days later, the agency sent Rebecca a wad of paperwork which she duly worked through before consulting an employment solicitor.

Her situation was complicated by the fact that, although she'd worked at the agency for seven years, she'd only had a permanent contract for three. Nevertheless, the solicitor assured Rebecca that she was entitled to more money than the agency were offering. Rebecca had to arrange two more meetings with the finance director before things were finally settled.

It was weird going back to the office where I'd worked for seven years. I'd just taken out a mortgage on my flat, so I was worried about my finances. As I'd already signed on, I knew that I was over-qualified for any advertising jobs that were going.

Rebecca found the meetings with the finance director difficult but she still managed to increase her severance payment by 50%. Once she'd signed a confidentiality agreement, her days in the advertising industry were over. A couple of years after she left, the agency went bankrupt so the staff who were still there received no compensation whatsoever.

Reflecting back on the experience, I feel lucky to have left when I did. It came at the right time because I was about to take my final exams and I already knew that counselling was my thing. It gave me a much needed push; I'd have found it difficult to take that step by myself.

Fortunately, Rebecca qualified for some self-employment training. She set up her own counselling company and gave herself the task of gaining accreditation and building up her client hours.

Fast forward to the beginning of 2010 and Rebecca was now working 35 hours as a counsellor in a large company. Even though she knew that redundancies were imminent, she didn't see herself as being in the at risk category. Until that is she found herself in a peculiarly inept occupational health group meeting.

The meeting got off to a bad start when a faulty projector took 20 minutes to fix. During the outage, the assembled employees had to congratulate a performance management assistant on her forthcoming marriage, even though most of them didn't know her from Adam.

When the meeting finally got off the ground, Rebecca and the rest of the counselling team discovered that a quarter of them would be leaving the organization, not because of redundancy – a word that the managers couldn't even bring themselves to utter, but because some of their work was being outsourced to an employee assistance programme (EAP). The managers presented this as a wholly positive move and completely failed to acknowledge any of the counselling team's concerns.

Rebecca was at a loss: the organization had spent the last two years building up the counselling team because of increasing demand, and the team still had more work than it could handle. She made this point in the meeting, but her concerns were brushed aside with a brusque:

If you've got any questions, speak to your line manager.

In Rebecca's case, this was a complete non-starter: her line manager just disappeared, conveniently finding reasons to be out of the office. She tried contacting HR; that turned out to be an impersonal black hole. Even when she finally managed to track down an alleged source of information – a folder on the departmental drive – it was empty.

This time, it was more of a shock, and I was much angrier. It was the combination of confusion, lack of information about even the most basic things such as procedures, timelines, next steps, dates of the next meeting and, of course, the total lack of transparency.

Bad as this backdrop was, it got worse. Not only was Rebecca struggling to come to terms with her own situation, she still had to counsel internal clients from other parts of the organization who were also facing redundancy.

When Rebecca received a form asking her to choose between either voluntary redundancy or staying in post, she refused to sign it because she simply didn't know which box to tick.

It was my way of holding onto a little bit of power because I felt so powerless.

Acknowledging to herself that she was buckling under the burden, Rebecca looked to her own resources. She channelled her frustration into creative poetry (see below), and paid for some private counselling because she knew that she needed external support.

The redundancy process dragged on for nine months; even those who accepted voluntary severance at the beginning had to stay for that period. In the end, Rebecca kept her job, but recognized that the effect on morale within the team was devastating. Perhaps even more devastating were the effects of this approach to redundancy on the wider organization.

The senior people thought they were doing us a favour by not giving us any information, but when you have to read between the lines, you automatically go to the worst case scenario. They seemed to think that if they were brutally honest, then we'd have got all emotional. We'd much rather have confronted the reality of redundancy than have it dressed up as good news about an employee assistance programme.

More worryingly for the health of the organization, the number of employees referring themselves to the group stress sessions run by the counselling team dropped dramatically. Rebecca attributes this to fear that they'll be singled out for redundancy if they admit to being under stress.

Rebecca is philosophical:

I see endings as new beginnings. People are much more adaptable than they realize. I've survived so far and I'll survive again. Just be aware that redundancy is a rollercoaster of emotions, so put as much support in place as you can.

One day at anyplc

my dept was up for sale.

Part buy, Part let

EAPs, place your bet.

'It's part of the process, it's in the mix.'

'Business as usual, there's no fix.'

Don't mention redundancies

It's voluntary severance you see.

Everyone's happy…justifiably

'It's part of the process, it's in the mix.'

'Business as usual, there's no fix.'

Meetings took place

PowerPoint disgrace.

This is no place

For weddings and lace.

'It's part of the process, it's in the mix.'

'Business as usual, there's no fix.'

Managers gone AWOL

The dept's left to fall

New policy, new system

Just adds to the friction

'It's not as we know it, time to mix.'

'Business as usual, find a fix.'

Chapter XXVIII

Will

Will is a personal development and training professional in his fifties. He'd been working for a multinational employer for over ten years when the axe fell.

You know all that best practice stuff about redundancy never coming as a shock. Well, you can forget all that. I was on long-term sick leave when Geoff, my line manager – and someone that I had tagged as a mate – invited me into the office for a friendly chat to see how I was doing. Even when I double-checked the purpose of the meeting, I still got that response.

What Will actually got was an all too typical confrontational redundancy meeting with Geoff and an unknown woman from HR. As far as Will's concerned, it had all the classic 'them and us' features: Will isolated on one side of the table facing the other two, Will being shut down every time he asked a question, Will being made to feel that he's no longer one of the tribe.

At this point in our interview, he suddenly throws back his head and starts laughing.

What's so funny?

I've never seen it this way before, but talking about it again makes me realize that it was a re-run of all that horrible stuff we go through in the playground as kids. You know those times when, for whatever reason, everyone else gangs up on you and you suddenly no longer belong, but you don't have a clue how you've transgressed. It's the absolutely perfect analogy, at least in my case.

Once Will realized that Geoff wasn't going to acknowledge their relationship or to engage with him beyond spouting a few perfunctory and predictable words about the current economic climate, he decided to keep the meeting short. He stayed just long enough to establish the basic facts and to try and explain to the HR manager that severance could only be 'voluntary' if he chose it by an act of will.

It was hopeless; in my playground analogy, the HR woman would be the spiteful six-year old. She kept asking me if I had any more questions; as her response was always 'that's confidential', I didn't see much point in persisting. I pride myself on being a learning animal.

As soon as he was outside the building, Will phoned his brother-in-law for the name of a good employment lawyer. He discussed everything with his wife and teenage children that evening, but he knew exactly what he was going to do.

First thing next morning, Will was in the lawyer's office, discussing his situation. By the time he left, he knew that he did have a case against his employer because the redundancy process had been less than perfect, but he also understood that he was running a risk. His employer could have refused his demands and simply included him in a compulsory redundancy programme at a later date and with even less financial compensation.

It was never about the money, but I knew that the company had a history of giving one month's pay for every year of service. The amount I'd been offered was way below that. I didn't give my employer permission to treat me disrespectfully in that conference room and I wasn't going to give it permission to disrespect my contribution by giving me less than I deserved. The money was just a proxy.

The lawyer made two remarks that helped Will enormously. He pointed out that the company wanted to get rid of Will, so it probably would agree to what he wanted. Second, Will had been stressing big time about the fact that his employer had only given him a week in which to accept voluntary severance or not. His lawyer told him it was completely irrelevant, so Will just forgot about it.

As it turned out, everything settled surprisingly quickly. Although Will's employer refused to accept that it had done anything wrong, it did agree to give him the extra money free of tax and to pay for his employment lawyer, on condition that he sign a confidentiality agreement. It also offered to give him a 'satisfactory' reference.

Judgemental or what? In all the years I'd been there, I'd never had anything lower than 'exceeds expectations' in my appraisals, but I only get a 'satisfactory' reference when I leave. I told them what to do with it. I already knew that I wouldn't be returning to corporate life.

Will readily admits that he found the whole experience extremely disturbing and that he and his family went through some difficult times. He'd done private coaching from time to time before, so he knew the general direction in which he was heading, but it still took time to adjust and to build up his network.

I got over the initial shock in about two weeks. I've done a lot of personal development work so I knew exactly what was happening on the inside. In many ways, it was worse for my family than it was for me. I was an unusual – and probably unwanted – presence in the house during daylight hours and I know that was difficult for my wife and kids. We also all had to get used to doing without things that we'd previously taken for granted.

Will now has a well-established business and seems remarkably at ease with himself and the world. I ask him if he has any regrets about leaving corporate life.

For myself, no. For my employer, yes. It got so much else so right that it saddens me deeply that it behaved the way it did at the point of departure. You don't get to your mid-fifties without having to confront some pretty dreadful stuff: unexpected illness, death of your parents. My employer supported me through all that in ways that still bring a lump to my throat. What's really sad is that I would have left willingly. All Geoff had to do was pick up the phone and say 'D'you want to talk about it?'.

I ask Will if he's seen Geoff since that meeting. He shakes his head; his sadness is palpable. I wonder aloud if it's because he still resents Geoff's behaviour. It isn't.

I'd previously coached one of the HR managers through her discomfort with the company's redundancy process so I knew exactly what was going on. The strategy consists of muzzling the line managers in case they say anything sympathetic, understanding or remotely human, so all you get is the HR bullshit – cold, calculating, compassionless.

I understand Geoff was under orders; I bear him no ill-will. And I'm certainly not going to carry away any negative emotion from that meeting. But do you seriously think he'd want me in his life? I'd just remind him of what is probably one of the lowest points of his career: sitting there without the balls to show up as a living, breathing human being or to stand up to an HR underling at least three grades lower down the hierarchy?

As the interview winds down, I pose my final question about what Will thinks he's learned.

As an older – but not necessarily wiser – member of the workforce, I know now that you don't have to be afraid of coming out from under the corporate umbrella. If you've been in it all your working life as I had, saying 'goodbye' to all the perks can be unsettling, but there's a whole strata of working life that goes on outside. I meet the most amazing people in networking and entrepreneur groups who earn their living in all sorts of weird and wacky ways. Many of them have been through the redundancy mill and come out the other side as their true selves.

Then Will roars with laughter again. I'm curious as to what it is that's set him off this time.

I've just found the analogy for that awful moment when you have to hand all your corporate paraphernalia back. When the security man stands over you ticking it all off a list: Blackberry – yes, laptop – yes, identity pass – yes. That's like those scenes in films when the criminals arrive at prison and have to empty their pockets and hand over their worldly goods.

It's arse about face because, in my case, the company wasn't taking my freedom away from me, it was giving it back. I, for one, am not handing that degree of control to anyone ever again. So there. Sorry to revert to the language of the playground, but that's where my employer left me.

Will grins broadly and we adjourn to the bar.

How This Book Doesn't End – Yet

Much is clearer to me now than it was when I started this book, but there's one word that dominates my list of realizations. When I see it, it's in 72 point bold type; when I hear it, it's through loud hailers; when I feel it, it's an overpowering sensation in the pit of my stomach. That word is:

CONVERSATION

In common with much else in this book, it's for both internal and external application. On the internal front, I've realized just how important it is for us to have a rich and regular conversation with ourselves. Asking ourselves those exacting but essential questions, such as:

Does this look/sound/feel right?

What do I want out of this?

Why do I do that?

Am I there yet?

can make a huge difference. Listening to – and acting on – the answers could be the difference that makes the difference to our life.

As for the external application, thinking about that takes me right back to the 18th June, 2010 and my redundancy meeting. Conversation was notable for its absence, not just in my meeting but in so many of the others that feature in this book. However, I now see those meetings from a completely different perspective.

Thanks to Annabel Kaye, I know that the representatives of HR and line management aren't the 'baddies'; they're just the other hapless players in a scene that is as disempowering for them as it is for the person being made redundant. Thanks to my conversations with Dorothy, Joanna and Murielle, I also know that HR – or at least the people who assume the HR role – can conduct redundancy compassionately and respectfully; can, in fact, live up to the 'h is for human' in human resources.

Sadly, for as long as we stick with the 'Trade Descriptions Act approach to redundancy' as Annabel so vividly calls it, I can't see much changing. The fact that I can't see the change isn't going to stop me from trying to make it happen. What's that quotation?

You must be the change you want to see in the world – Mahatma Gandhi.

Tall order? Yes. Impossible? Not in my map of the world. As it says at the very beginning of this book:

Watch out, watch out – there's a Redundancy Crusader about!

References

1 Philpott J (2012), 'Counting the Cost of the Jobs Recession' p 3-4; 'Work Audit' (March 2012); London: CIPD

2 Ready R & Burton K (2004), 'Neuro-linguistic Programming for Dummies'; Chichester: John Wiley & Sons, Ltd

3 International Teaching Seminars: www.itsnlp.com; info@itsnlp.com; + 44 (0) 1268 777125

4 Carr N (2008), 'Is Google Making Us Stupid?'; published in 'The Atlantic' (July 2008)

5 Lopez SJ (2008), 'Positive Psychology: Discovering Human Strengths' p 136-140; Westport, CT: Praeger Publishers Inc

6 Mosing MA, Zietsch BP, Shekar SN, Wright MJ & Martin NG (2009), 'Genetic and Environmental Influences on Optimism and its Relationship to Mental and Self-Rated Health: A Study of Ageing Twins'; published online: 18 July 2009 Springer Science + Business Media, LLC

7 Seligman MEP (2006), 'Learned Optimism: How to Change Your Mind and Your Life'; New York: Simon & Schuster

8 Seligman MEP (2007), 'Authentic Happiness', p 93; London: Nicholas Brearley Publishing

9 King James Bible (1611), Proverbs 17:22

10 Miller M, Mangano C, Park Y, Goel R, Plotnick GD & Vogel RA (2006), 'Impact of Cinematic Viewing on Endothelial Function'; published in 'Heart' (2006 Feb;92(2):261-2)

11 Bennett MP, Zeller JM, Rosenberg L, & McCann J (2003), 'The Effect of Mirthful Laughter on Stress and Natural Killer Cell Activity'; published in 'Alternative Therapies in Health and Medicine' (9 (2), 38-45)

[12] Smith LB (1990), 'Humor Relations for Nurse Managers'; published in 'Nursing Management' (21, 86)

[13] Copyrighted by Values in Action Institute under the direction of Christopher Peterson and Martin EP Seligman

[14] Miller GA, Galanter E, & Pribram KH (1960), 'Plans and the Structure of Behaviour'; New York: Holt, Rinehart & Winston

[15] Korzybski AH (1933), 'Science and Sanity: An Introduction to non-Aristotelian Systems and General Semantics'

[16] Fredericks M (2005), 'Head Games', p 104; London: Simon & Schuster UK Ltd

[17] Muraven M, Tice DM, & Baumeister RF (1998), 'Self-control as limited resource: regulatory depletion patterns'; published in 'Journal of Personality and Social Psychology' (volume: 74, Issue: 3, publisher: American Psychological Association p 774-89)

[18] Wallace D (2003), 'Join Me: The True Story of a Man who Started a Cult by Accident'; London: Ebury Press; Wallace D (2004), 'Random Acts of Kindness: 365 Ways to Make the World a Nicer Place'; London: Ebury Press

[19] Shore DM & Heerey EA, School of Psychology, Bangor University (2011), 'The value of genuine and polite smiles'; published in 'Emotion', February 2011

[20] King James Bible (1611), Acts 20:35

[21] Williams N (2011), 'Resisting Your Soul' by Nick Williams, p 33; Brenzett: Balloon View Ltd

[22] International Teaching Seminars: www.itsnlp.com; nfo@itsnlp.com; + 44 (0) 1268 777125

[23] i3 Profiling: www.i3profiling.com; info@i3profiling.com; + 44 (0) 79 4958 7497

[24] Copyrighted by Values in Action Institute under the direction of Christopher Peterson and Martin EP Seligman

[25] Seligman MEP (2007), 'Authentic Happiness', p 161; London: Nicholas Brearley Publishing

[26] BBC2 (13 March 2012), 'Horizon'

[27] McDermott I & Shircore I (1999), 'Manage Yourself, Manage Your Life' p 127; London: Piatkus

[28] I trained with Matt Ferguson of Motivation Training: www.motivationtraining.co.uk; info@motivationtraining.co.uk; + 44 (0) 1479 831614

[29] International Teaching Seminars: www.itsnlp.com; info@itsnlp.com; + 44 (0) 1268 777125

[30] www.wildmind.org

[31] International Teaching Seminars: www.itsnlp.com; info@itsnlp.com; + 44 (0) 1268 777125

[32] www.oxforddictionaries.com

[33] BBC2 (13 March 2012), 'Horizon'

[34] The Walt Disney Company (1966), 'Winnie-the-Pooh and the Honey Tree'

Glossary

Anchoring	Associating one thing with another so as to provoke a response. Anchors move us from one *state* to another and can be in any of the three main *representational systems.*
As if frame	Thinking or acting as if we have already have the necessary resource(s).
Association	Being fully engaged with our own experience – whether in the past, present or future – by using all our senses.
Behaviour	All human activity including both voluntary and involuntary processes; one of the *logical levels.*
Behavioural flexibility	Realizing that we always have more than one choice.
Beliefs	Subjective ideas about ourselves, our world and how we relate to it; one of the *logical levels.*
Capability	A skill that can be broken down into its component parts, can be part of a *strategy,* and can enable us to achieve an *outcome;* one of the *logical levels.*
Chunking	Grouping information by class by moving up or down a level and thereby changing our relationship to it.

263

Congruence	The state of being in *rapport* with ourselves.
Conscious	Everything of which we are aware in the here and now.
Dissociation	Being outside of our own experience, as if we are at one remove from it.
Environment	The context in which we operate, including time, place and people; one of the *logical levels.*
First position	Being aware of the external world from our individual point of view only.
Fourth position	Perceiving the world from the viewpoint of the other three positions.
Future pacing	Mental rehearsal during which we place new *behaviours, capabilities* and perceptions into our future so that we can draw on them as appropriate.
Identity	How we see, hear and feel about ourselves; one of the *logical levels.*
Incongruence	The state of being out of *rapport* with ourselves.
In time	A *timeline* pattern with the past behind us, the future in front of us, and 'now' running through our body.
Kinaesthetic	Relating to feeling, touch, sensations – both in real and remembered time.
Logical levels	Content categories relating to different levels of experience: *behaviour, beliefs, capabilities, environment, identity, spiritual self.*

Map of the world	Our unique way of representing the world to ourselves, based on our individual experience and perceptions.
Matching	Respectfully mirroring another person's *behaviour, beliefs, capabilities* in order to build *rapport.*
Modal operator of necessity	Words such as *should must, ought, have to* that denote requirement.
Modelling	Adopting *the behaviours, beliefs, capabilities, strategies* of another person so as to build a model of how they do what they do.
Outcome	What we want expressed and experienced in very specific sensory-based terms.
Outcome orientation	Knowing what we want and checking that we're using appropriate behaviour to achieve it.
Pacing and leading	Meeting other people in their *map of the world*, and then establishing and building *rapport* with them so that they follow us.
Positive intention	The positive purpose behind our *behaviours* and *beliefs.*
Presuppositions	*Beliefs* and *values* that are so ingrained that we take them for granted and act upon them – often outside of conscious awareness.
Rapport	A harmonious and understanding relationship with ourselves and with others.

Reframing	Thinking about things in a different way by adopting a different frame or perspective.
Representational systems	The systems we use to re-present information to ourselves on the inside; known as VAKOG where V = visual, A = auditory, K = kinaesthetic, O = olfactory and G = gustatory.
Resource	Anything that contributes to achieving an *outcome*.
Role model	Another being who has *behaviours, beliefs* or *capabilities* that we would like to develop.
Second position	Being aware of the external world from another person's perspective and understanding that perspective to some extent.
Self-limiting beliefs	Beliefs that limit what's possible for us; often taken on from authority figures during childhood; often expressed using *universal quantifiers.*
Sensory acuity	Noticing the effects of what we do, on ourselves and on others.
Spiritual self	A higher level of experience in which we have stepped fully into ourselves and our life's purpose; one of the *logical levels.*
State	The sum total of our physical well-being, thoughts and emotions. Our state affects us on a neurological, physical, mental, emotional, energetic and spiritual level.

Strategy	A sequence of mental and physical processes that we can repeat consistently to produce a specific *outcome*.
Submodalities	The building blocks of the five senses such as black and white or colour for visual; mono or stereo for auditory.
Third position	Being aware of the external world from a completely neutral perspective.
Through time	A *timeline* pattern with the line passing somewhere in front of us.
Timeline	A line that we use to represent the passage of time from our past to our future, using images, sounds and feelings.
TOTE	A self-correcting feedback loop consisting of Test, Operate, Test, Exit.
Trance	An altered *state* of consciousness during which our attention is firmly focused inwards; commonly known as 'being away with the fairies'.
Trigger event	A past event which we may not consciously remember but which nonetheless leads us into an unresourceful *state*.
Unconscious	Everything of which we are not aware in the here and now.
Universal quantifier	Words that denote totality such as *never, nobody, all, ever, everybody.*

Values   The principles according to which we lead our
                       lives; these can be in or out of our conscious
                       awareness.

Well-formedness   The six conditions that ensure that an *outcome*
conditions   is well formed and therefore workable and
                       ecological for us.

About the Author

Elaine Hopkins morphed into the Redundancy Crusader in 2012. Morphing has been something of a theme in her life. Before her latest incarnation, she'd already morphed from:

- an unresourceful human being into 'the most resourceful person I know', to quote her father;

- a corporate copywriter into a coach;

- a full-time employee into a freelance portfolio career woman.

None of these transitions would have been possible for Elaine without the transformative power of neuro-linguistic programming (NLP) which she discovered in 2004. Inspired by the profound changes she had been able to make in her own life and by her passion to help others to develop themselves, Elaine achieved, over the course of the next six years, formal qualifications as a master NLP practitioner, accredited NLP coach, certified hypnotherapist and dyslexia coach.

In 2010, Elaine experienced redundancy for the first time – after 35 years in corporate life. It was both a shock and a turning point. If Elaine has one outstanding skill, it's the ability to get straight to the heart of the matter, often by the use of 'razor-sharp questioning'. And this is a skill that she has deployed to good effect to get to grips with what's really going on with redundancy.

Elaine took a year out of her own post-redundancy journey to investigate. She interviewed not just the theoretical, technical experts, but the practical ones as well: people who'd been through the experience and come out the other side. This book is the result: a unique blend of Elaine's coaching and copywriting skills, informed by her insights into corporate life, and focused in an entirely practical way on helping those who have been made redundant to help themselves.

Elaine's crusade is far from over; in the short-term, she's totally committed to helping all those of you who are affected by redundancy to get over the experience and get on with the rest of your life. In the longer-term, her quest is to identify, or create, if necessary, a better model of redundancy than the one currently in use. Here's all you need to keep up-to-date with the latest tips, tools and techniques:

www.redundancycrusader.co.uk (with free download)

www.redundancywithrespect.com (with free downloads)

Facebook: Redundancy Crusader

LinkedIn: Elaine Hopkins

Twitter: @elaine_hopkins

YouTube: Elaine Hopkins.

Index

ABCDE model, 23

Anchoring, 7, 61, 76

Aristotle, 126

As if frame, 83

Association, 61, 73, 102, 149

Bandler, Richard, 7

Baseline state, 30-31

Behaviour, 7, 14, 47, 49, 73, 76, 84,
86, 88, 99, 102-103, 109, 115, 129,
138, 153-155, 168, 171-172, 174-
176

Behavioural flexibility, 7, 60, 79-87,
158, 169

Beliefs, 23, 49-51, 53, 55-56, 69, 170

Capability, 170-171

Carey, Mariah, 70

Change personal history, 102, 105

Chunking, 163

Circle of excellence, 74, 102, 105

Clash, 115

Cognitive dissonance, 191-192

Comfort zone, 21, 79, 87-88

Communication, 60-62, 127, 157,
161-164, 185-186, 204

Competence, 170

Competitiveness, 66

Congruence, 140, 165

Conscious, 120-127, 164-165

Corporate life, 13, 101, 105, 110-
115, 124, 145, 160, 211, 253-254

Curiosity, 8, 83-84

Dawson, Les, 28

Descartes, René, 28, 120

Disaster scenario planning, 145-148,
152

Dissociation, 61, 73

Dyslexia, 2, 56

Eeyore, 24, 174

Eggheads, 120

Ellison, Larry, 50

Environment, 171

Erikson, Milton, 7

Exams, 70, 149-150

Failure, 10, 74, 76, 95-96, 133, 174

Feedback, 10, 34-35, 76, 114, 125,
132, 135, 172-176

First position, 42, 44-46

Fourth position, 43-44

Fowler, Daphne, 120

Future pacing, 75, 102, 153

Gandhi, Mahatma, 258

Gershwin, George, 29

Grinder, John, 7

Hart, Miranda, 76

Health, 22, 24, 122, 138

Henderson, Grant, 113

Horizon, 119, 167

HR function, 187-192

Humour, 46, 95, 112, 114, 133

Identity, 14, 56, 89, 93, 109, 170-172, 189, 211

Imagination, 8, 43, 73, 83, 128, 136, 178-179

In time, 90-93

Incompetence, 170

Incongruence, 140-141, 165, 171

Information, 39-40, 65, 114-115, 118, 120, 123, 125, 128, 149, 160, 164, 173-177

Inklings, 119-128

Interview technique, 34, 62-65, 72, 91

Jackson 5, 70

Kabat-Zinn, Jon, 128

Kettering, Charles F, 179

Kinaesthetic, 38-41, 57-58, 60, 93, 144, 161

Language, 38, 44, 57, 75, 95, 124, 140, 150, 158-159, 161

Laughter, 22-24

Law, 183

Lloyd, Marie, 18

Logical levels, 170, 172

Machine code, 90, 102-103, 149

Map of the world, 37, 41, 45, 49, 144, 157-158, 164

Matching, 162

McDermott, Ian, 7, 30, 137

Meta-mirror, 42- 47, 85, 175

Memory, 8, 32, 38, 70, 90, 100, 102-103, 149, 178, 209

Mindfulness, 128

Mirroring, 158

Modal operators of necessity, 65, 73, 86, 146

New behaviour generator, 153-155

NLP, 2, 6-9, 32-33, 37-38, 40, 42, 55, 65, 69, 70, 73, 76, 80, 84, 87, 89, 95, 102, 103, 106, 114, 126, 130, 133, 137, 140, 144, 155, 157, 158, 161, 163, 170, 172

Outcome, 34-35, 43, 69, 76, 88, 130-141, 164, 174

Outcome orientation, 7, 130, 132, 158

Pacing and leading, 162

Performance management, 188, 190, 205

Perls, Fritz, 7

Perspective, 25-26, 42-47, 61, 80, 85, 93, 105, 160

Plasticity, 167

Positive by-product, 137-138

Positive intention, 99, 138

Positive Psychology, 6, 23

Preferences, 39, 113, 163

Presuppositions, 7-8, 72-73, 87

Profiling, 113

Random acts of kindness, 81

Rapport, 7, 73, 133, 157-165

Redundancy, 1-9, 13, 18, 19, 21, 24-25, 29, 32, 50, 53, 62, 79, 90, 99, 109-110, 130, 167, 178, 183, 184-216, 221, 223, 225, 228-229, 232-258

Reframing, 7,50, 76, 150, 153

Relationship with ourselves, 57, 59

Representational (rep) systems, 7, 38-40, 57, 60, 121, 134, 140, 144, 146-148, 159-162

Resources, 44, 69-76, 93, 102, 105, 133, 135, 167

Role model, 10, 21, 31, 41, 73-74, 85, 135, 153-155, 163, 169

Role modelling, 73, 84, 153

Satir, Virginia, 7

Second position, 43-44, 135

Self-compassion, 67

Self-limiting beliefs, 50, 55, 73, 86

Seligman, Martin, 6, 23, 114

Sensory acuity, 7, 35, 76, 121, 158-159, 174

Simonton, Carl, 22

Slack, 25, 67, 145, 211

Small, Heather, 77

Smoking, 131, 133, 137-140

Spice Girls, 129

Spiritual self, 172

State, 22, 27-34, 44, 49-50, 59, 69, 74-75, 97, 125, 147, 149, 169, 174, 177

Stone, Lew, 10

Strategy, 76, 133, 144-150, 153

Submodalities, 57-60, 147

Supremes, 147

System, 19-20, 24, 28, 38-40, 49, 57, 60, 103, 113, 121, 135, 139-140, 144-145, 147, 171, 175

Third position, 43, 44

Thoreau, Henry David, 125

Through time, 90-93

Timeline, 9, 89-97, 101, 102, 105-106, 117-118

TOTE model, 34, 141

Trance, 123-125, 128

Transition, 15-19, 22-26, 79, 145

Treats, 18, 67

Trigger event, 100, 102-105

Twain, Mark, 23

Unconscious, 53, 72-73, 85, 117-119, 122, 127, 168, 170

Universal quantifiers (Universals), 64-65, 73, 86

Values, 49, 112, 115, 121, 140, 170

Values in Action surveys, 6, 31, 114

Voices, 57, 59, 146-147, 151, 153

Wallace, Danny, 81

Well-formedness conditions, 133

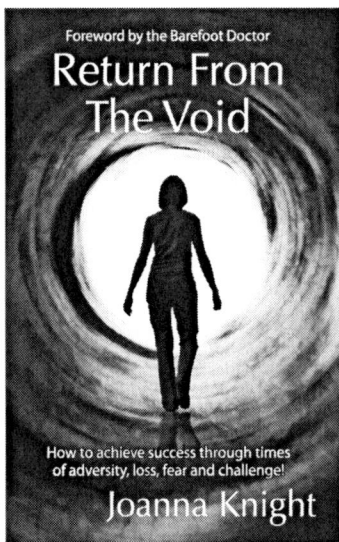

Return From The Void

How to achieve success through times
of adversity, loss, fear and challenge!

by Joanna Knight

*Available from Amazon and
www.liveitpublishing.com*

When You Think You Have Lost Everything... Think Again!

Based on her challenging and adverse personal experiences, combined with professional knowledge: Clinical Hypnotherapist and Stress Consultant Joanna Knight gives you her own unique insight, direction and philosophy into a tried and tested recipe for mental well-being, happiness and on-going success!

Learn how to:

Create room for mistakes to initiate growth   Notice fresh opportunities

Gain motivation, focus and clarity   Find out what you want

Release self-limiting patterns and beliefs   Discover your true potential

Discover your own truth with new awareness   Gain a powerful new perspective

Make your world work for you!

"What I love about this book is that it takes into account that people are busy and want to get to the point quickly. Joanna does this, successfully blending candid, personal experience with simple yet extremely powerful methods to transform your life. Joanna's message is clear – if she can go from losing everything to gaining a life of happiness, health and success, so can you!"
Murielle Maupoint, Author of The Essential NLP Practitioner's Handbook.

"Joanna has taught me that through adversity you can rise from a 'Bottomless Pit' and come back 'Triumphantly'. Not only has she accomplished this, she has courageously written this for others to show them the way through!"
Liz Everett, Healer & Author of An Inner Light That Shines So Bright.

Despite following the advice of a wealth of best-selling self-help books, most of us still struggle to understand the fundamental laws and principles that govern the universe, our interactions within it and our ability to achieve success, health, wealth and happiness.

Have you ever wondered why the Law of Attraction doesn't work for you?

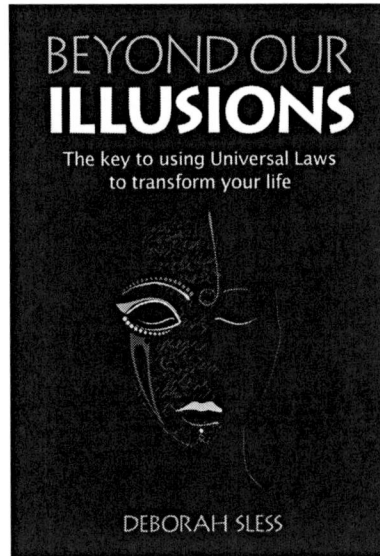

BEYOND OUR ILLUSIONS

The key to using Universal Laws to transform your life

DEBORAH SLESS

The answer is simple: The Universal Laws <u>cannot</u> *work in your favour until you identify and remove the psychological issues that are blocking your ability to live the life you want.*

In her ground breaking and easy-to-understand book, psychotherapist Deborah Sless, uses the concrete psychological theory of Transactional Analysis to uncover the secrets of the Universal Laws. **Beyond Our Illusions** takes you on a journey of self-discovery to understand:

- The Universal Laws and how they impact our lives
- Your own individual Life Story and the beliefs that were formed in childhood
- How to achieve freedom from your illusions and master your self
- The concept of Spirit as an energy force and how to tap into it

Genuine self-development is not easy but Deborah Sless provides her readers with the tools and framework they need - through clear explanations, examples and exercises - to begin a journey of self-discovery and change toward ultimate fulfilment.

ISBN: 978-1-906954-42-0
Publication: 1 August 2012

Format: Paperback
RRP: £14.99

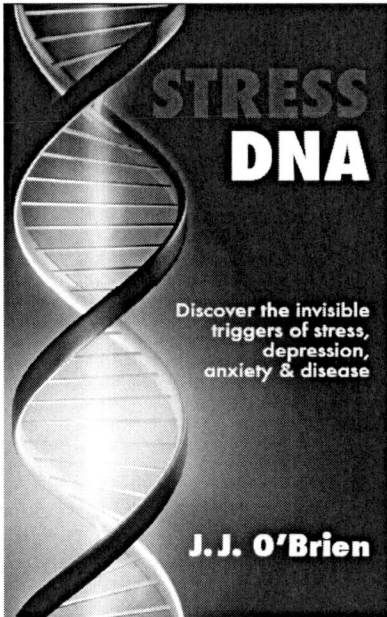

Discover a new wealth of knowledge about the nature and causes of stress and stress related conditions.

In this compelling book, J.J.O'Brien takes you on a personal and professional journey that many people have already described as being a profoundly absorbing and a life changing read.

Alongside this journey, Stress DNA offers a new understanding of The Subconscious, unlocks The Emotional Void and shows how The Transformation Periods all impact on our lives and allows stress to invade.

This book breaks down the causes of stress and clearly shows how stress is formed internally in the mind and emotions. This is a book of understanding, a way of thinking to change your way of being.

"I read this book when I was starting the menopause and not only was I full of understanding but the chapter on The Transformation Periods helped me to take the stress out of an emotionally troublesome time for me. So impressed was I on reading the book that I immediately ordered a copy for all of my family members." (B.B.)

ISBN: 978-1-906954-40-6   **Format: Paperback**

Lightning Source UK Ltd.
Milton Keynes UK
UKOW010416020812

196929UK00003B/15/P